VIGNETTES OF A BIRDER

by
Pamela Conley

ISBN: 1500998796
ISBN 13: 9781500998790
Library of Congress Control Number: 2014915770
CreateSpace Independent Publishing Platform
North Charleston, South Carolina

Front cover art work was done by my husband, Dennis Beall.

Beall has worked in all printmaking media, including intaglio, lithography, collagraph, relief, screenprint, and monoprint. His work has been featured in over 30 solo exhibitions, and over 300 national and international exhibitions. His work is held in numerous collections private and public, national and international.

This book is dedicated to the birds who guided me to my passion, to my travels, and to my husband.

And it is also dedicated to my husband, Dennis Beall, who without his support, this book would never have been written.

ACKNOWLEDGEMENTS

First I want to thank my husband, Dennis, for the support and the cover art and illustrations he produced for this book.

Thank you, my friend, Ann Shadwick, for your support and first read through editing this book.

I also would like to thank my first mentors who gave me the passion for birding, the late Arnold Small, and late Robert Arbib.

Thank you, Cheryl Morris, for accepting the job and doing an excellent job editing this book.

Thank you Debbie Crammer and Mary Anne Sobieraj for offering to do the last final reads before submission.

I also would like to thank my long-time friend, Ron Moore, for his support and his answering my endless questions regarding how to get this to publication.

Introduction

After the discovery and passion has begun to take wing, the evolution of a birder begins, and the life of a birder is forever changed. I was 26 years old and a flight attendant when I discovered these flying jewels. My eyes opened up, and it was like seeing the Milky Way for the first time. Not only did I spend time prowling the beaches and woods near my home in Manhattan Beach, California, but I discovered a new dimension to my travels as a flight attendant.

I met my soul-mate while birding, which brought me to northern California where we settled in a small redwood community near the Russian River.

I left the travel industry and began working in Bodega Bay at a small taffy store selling T-shirts and candy to the tourists. The taffy store had a window looking over the bay where I could bird-watch while working. It was soon after I began working there that I began to write a weekly birding column for the *Bodega Bay Navigator*. Over the next 12 years, I never missed a deadline or tired of writing about the birds.

After moving to the redwoods, we soon became involved in battles with the California Department of Forestry over timber harvest plans. Again, saving trees was deeply connected to our passion for birds and their connection to everything we loved. It doesn't matter what political persuasion a birder may be, I have never met a birder who wasn't deeply committed to protecting the environment.

I may be one of the few bird watchers who still doesn't own an IPod because I can't imagine missing the calls of the birds and knowing the identities of those calls on my walks. A walk to the compost pit or to take the trash out always becomes an excuse to listen or watch for birds.

Once the passion for bird-watching captured my heart, everything changed. It brought forth the poet in me, involved me in politics and the environment, took me on trips far away in pursuit of seeing the unusual, introduced me to my soul-mate, and even saved my life once.

The Vignettes of a Birder is about the evolution of my life after the passion for birds took flight.

I'm hopeful these short journeys, meditations, and reflections will bring other birders moments to reflect on their own involvement with nature and how birding changed their lives.

Birds connect us to nature, to freedom, to flight and to song. Without their color, the world would be bleak and dull. Without their flight, our fantasies would be limited.

Without their song, the silence would be unbearable.

The Beginning

Majestic glaciers

Towering spires of blue ice

Eagles soaring high

Bird-Watching Beginnings

I became a birdwatcher the day my ex-husband's father took me out to show me the world of birding. The day began at 8 am and ended at 6 pm. At the end of the day, we had seen 75 species, and I was hooked. It was hard to believe there were so many birds I had not noticed before. I enjoyed the hunt for these precious feathered jewels.

My marriage was slowly deteriorating, and I found myself turning more to birding to get away. I discovered that being outdoors and developing the skills of birding was healing the emotional scars caused by grief and disappointment in my marriage. Birding brought me new friends outside of my marriage. I took weekend trips to various bird spots with the Audubon Society and American Birding Association. Birding made me stronger and finally I took flight too.

Birding was responsible for releasing me from one bad marriage and for bringing me my soul-mate and husband for the past 33 years into my life. We met in Colorado on an American Birding Association workshop and field trip to study the Rocky Mountain Birds. I flew into Denver and caught a ride to Fort Collins in the back of a farmer's pickup truck. It was arranged for me to ride with Dennis in his truck for the following four days. We were to ride herd behind the other cars to keep the stragglers together. As it turned out, we kept losing the others so enamored we were with each other. It cost me a life-bird, the red crossbill, and took me 10 years to add it to my list. I missed a bird, but gained a mate. It was worth the wait!

I think back at how ironic it was that fateful day my ex-husband's father opened the door and showed me the world of birding. I wonder where my life would be now had I not accepted that invitation to go with him. Birding changed the direction of my life and continues to change my life. I am now combining my passions for birding, traveling, and writing.

Birding at Work

This is taken from my first published article, which appeared in the Los Angeles Audubon Society's Western Tanager in March 1982. I was an International Flight Attendant at the time flying to Hawaii, Australia, and New Zealand.

As an International Flight Attendant, I am often asked by my fellow birding friends, "My, what a long life list you must have, being able to travel to all those exotic destinations." When birders take off on a jet plane, they usually have several weeks to spend birding intensely and come back with an endless list of birds, sunburn, and maybe with a few mosquito bites. Usually, if I'm lucky, I'll have a day or two at the most in one place and sometimes only 12 hours. When we do get to a rest stop, that is what we want to do most at that time – REST. What with time changes, 16-hour duty days, flying all night, all I want to do is take off my shoes and go to bed.

Birders on vacation usually take off with their cameras, binoculars, tripod, telescope, and at least ten field manuals. Try to pack all you need to look glamorous and add your binoculars, camera, and at least two field guides to one small suitcase, one garment bag, and one purse, and you might have some idea why I hate to pack for a trip. My union has not negotiated porters for us, and we still have to carry everything to and from the airport. Forget that souvenir sheepskin this trip, I sigh to myself.

But besides being a tired flight attendant with sore feet, I am also one of those crazy birders who will try anything to see new birds. I've often wondered if I'm the only birder in the world at times. No one I know in my profession shares this joy, and sometimes I must admit I feel like a misfit. Many times I'll be sitting on the crew bus headed for the airport, and we will pass a great flock of water birds. Instinctively I have yelled out, "Stop the bus!" – only to receive some grim frowns and rather unpleasant comments. I now sit by the window intently looking out with my hand over my mouth. The rest of the world really does think that all bird-watchers are little old ladies in tennis shoes.

Occasionally, I will rally to a great cause. The Hawaii Audubon often has field trips, and I decided to go one Sunday morning. I arrived in Honolulu at midnight and got up at 6:00 am. It was a marvelous day filled with many surprises and some new birds. We visited the red-footed booby nesting colony, and I added to my list a European widgeon, ricebird, and white-capped noddy. However, the day continued on until 7 pm, and when I got back to the hotel, I just had enough time to take a shower and get ready to go to the airport to fly home all night. It was one of the longest nights of my life.

As you can see, there are a lot of misconceptions about being a birder and the glamour of flying as a flight attendant. Besides suffering from jet lag and sore feet most of the time, I have had to learn to ignore disapproving remarks and raised eyebrows from my fellow employees. I've had to learn how to pack a suitcase exceptionally well to fit all the necessary equipment to bird and leave room for the hair dryer too. Combining my job and birding does have its hazards but has its advantages too. You see, I just added a New Zealand kingfisher to my life list.

After reading this and reflecting, I realized at the time I was catching the birding fever, few young women were interested in bird-watching. Most of the women interested in birds really were little old ladies in tennis shoes.

However, young single men interested in natural history were intensely caught up in the chase for birds. I may have been considered an outcast by my peers, but besides finding my passion for birds, I also found my passionate and life-time partner, my husband. I'm glad I followed my instincts and my own path.

My Birding Mentors

When I first started birding, I was alone.

My ex-father-in-law had opened up a new world to me, and then he disappeared as usual, taking off for another exotic destination. Armed with binoculars and a bird book, I stumbled through the process of learning to use these tools as well as a new taxonomy.

However, it was one jolly round man who made my birding experiences soar. In 1975, I took an extension class at UCLA on California Birds, taught by Arnold Small. Arnold was one of the front-runners chasing California birds. His bird photography was stunning and well respected. He was a major name in the California birding world for more than 50 years. His creativity as a teacher made it difficult to get into one of his UCLA classes.

The class was one night a week for six weeks with four weekend outings. Our text was his book *The Birds of California*, based on the many different California habitats and where to find the birds. I still have my signed copy and value it greatly for the memories it inspires.

It was on one of our class field trips to Mt. Pinos that I saw my one and only endangered condor. At the time, there were only about 30 left in the world. We had spent the day birding and were all disappointed we hadn't seen one. It was late afternoon, and we were preparing to eat, when I heard Arnold yell out, "Condor!"

Still wearing my binoculars, I looked up immediately and saw an enormous vulture sail close overhead. Only a few students saw it because the others had put their binoculars down to eat.

On one of these outings, Arnold asked me about my job. I told him I was a flight attendant, and he became quite excited. He asked if I had pass privileges, and he said I should start participating in the American Birding Association (ABA) extended weekend field trips offered in all parts of the United States. He suggested that I come to the ABA Convention in Texas in May.

I followed his suggestion and went to that convention – and to many other ABA weekend trips. Arnold was my birding mentor who introduced me not only to the California birds but to the opportunities of traveling the world in the chase for birds.

It was at that ABA Convention back in 1975 that I met another birding mentor. Not knowing a soul but Arnold, I boarded a bus and took a seat. A middle-age man with a mustache, glasses and a beret asked if anyone was sitting next to me. I said no – and thus began an exciting adventure with a new friend.

He wore a gray sweatshirt with a photo of Audubon on it. We immediately began talking, and I soon found out I was sitting with Robert Arbib, the editor of American Birding Magazine. He had also written the book *The Lord's Woods*, which won the John Burroughs Medal of American Museum of Natural History in 1972. He had a twinkle in his eye, a quick sense of humor, and a passion for birding and life.

For the next several days, he led me through the magic of migration as hundreds of eastern spring warblers fell from the sky tired and exhausted after their long journey flying over the Gulf. Through the passion of Arnold and Robert, I felt the heart-beating excitement and adrenaline rush as I watched in amazement those brilliant colored birds. Robert was always by my side, helping me identify them.

A couple of weeks later after my return home, I received a package in the mail. It was a gray Audubon sweatshirt, and a signed copy of his book. We kept a correspondence going for several years. It wasn't until I was married to Dennis that I actually saw Robert Arbib again. He was traveling through Northern California. Dennis and I drove down to Palo Alto and picked him up and brought him to our home for dinner.

Dennis and Robert became fast friends. We were both sad to hear of his passing a few years later in 1987 to a short illness.

I feel privileged to have known both of these important men who contributed so much to the world of birding.

Desert Visions

I was born into a family of desert rats who chose to live in a desert eventually invaded by orange grove trees. Later, tract homes invaded the orange grove trees, and my memory of their sweet-scented blossoms died with the sound of machines tearing roots and limbs apart.

My family's idea of fun was to wander through ghost towns, listening to the winds I imagined to be calling phantoms from the past.

My grandfather found a shiny glass shoe to fill with flowers. The edge of the glass sparkled purple in the sun, catching his eye. My uncle found a glass vinegar vessel; unbroken, it had turned purple from the sun – precious purple glass, perhaps tossed from a wagon, lost in time.

My family collected these treasures from the desert. I collected memories of barren wastelands, haunting winds that frightened me at night, and unbearable hellish heat without air conditioning. And I longed for the sound of foghorns, the smell of salty seas, and fine white sand between my toes, not unlike desert sand but cooler.

My forced journeys into the desert made me see it as an arid land, seducing dreamers with empty promises that turned them into desperados with deserted dreams.

I despised the yellow billboard signs beckoning travelers to Injun Joe's Trading Post with cement tepees painted cheap bright colors, not unlike the bad western movies of the fifties.

Rubbish piles of rusted refrigerators, carburetors, and ruined automobiles rested in their uncovered graves while dusty, rosy rocks matched the rust remains at sunset.

Two six-foot cracked Japanese Warriors, used as rifle targets, guarded the relic of an abandoned windblown shack. Distorted dreams that turned into dry boards sagging from their nails.

Wind howled louder than coyotes. Dust storms not discriminating, dusted everything with soft blankets of fine sand.

Roads with names led to no houses and empty bank accounts and broken dreams.

Painted bubblegum-pink like their lipstick, the Angel Ladies Brothel awaited the next drifter. Cheap perfume and pleasures came with a cheap price.

Dry salty lakes white with alkaline gave illusions of quivering wet lakes. The desert delivered delusions of false promises once again.

These were the memories I collected. My only fondness were the horny toads and desert tortoises that became my friends.

Eventually, I grew up and gained my independence from the desert rats. I moved next to the seashore and became a crab of solitude.

Solitude became lonely, and I began searching for a partner. I met my soul-mate while watching prairie falcons screaming mating calls on the Pawnee Grasslands of Colorado. He asked me to travel in his truck and see the desert through his eyes. It seemed I had fallen in love with another desert rat.

It was through his eyes and the words of Edward Abbey that I began to see a land formed by cataclysmic upheaval thousands of years ago. Small hills piled with pillars of rock – prehistoric explosions must have sent rocks bursting upwards into the sky to fall randomly where they are today.

Red formations reminded me of stupas in Thailand, Mayan ruins in Tikal, giant European cathedrals, Egyptian pyramids, and medieval castles.

Rocks blazed red against blue sky. A land created before dinosaurs, ancient and still evolving. The energy was powerful and strong. Perhaps it was created to remind us we are no bigger or smaller than a red ant in the macrocosm of life.

We awoke to the sweet, descending call of canyon wren. We sat in the cool shade as the broiling sun reached high noon, sharing our spot with lazy Chihuahua whiptail lizards. The pungent smell of released nitrogen in the air permeated the hot concrete, while big rain splatter cooled the hot earth and us.

I watched black-billed magpies fly randomly like the recent hatch of a black and white Weidemeyer's admiral butterflies, tails of ribbons streaming in the air.

Large brown tummies, rumpled with rolls, hung over hind feet, as prairie dogs stood up with wrinkled curious noses – then dove into their holes in haste as one lean coyote searched their city for an easy meal.

A large diamond-back rattled a warning and then went back to sleep under a rock. The silk scales glistened, each individual one shining like a glass bead.

After driving through miles of bleak brown landscape, we came upon a green oasis where we stopped for lunch and shade. A covey of Chukar took off from a spring of dripping water. We ate hurriedly as a family of curious antelopes stood on a slope above us, waiting and watching with huge brown eyes fringed with dark lashes. Their disturbing pleading calls reminded us that we were trespassing and they were thirsty.

After weeks of journeying through this land, we turned towards the mountains and camped near a blue lake. The sound of yellow-headed and red-winged blackbirds gurgling their water music began to wash away the anxiety I had felt in this foreign land.

My mate, the desert rat, had shown me the raw red beauty of the desert at sunset. We had tasted the sand on our skin and smelled the ozone of lightning strike before the thunderous booms followed with splattering rain.

But a crab can only stay away from water so long before it dies. I returned to the beach, and my mate followed me.

Each spring the desert calls my mate, and we return to the desert he taught me to love.

Bodega Bay

Tide pools filled with life

imprisoned and then released

Rhythms of the moon

The Taffy Store

I told my boss, "I'm going to make your day and mine. Goodbye."
The move to the new office had not gone well. In order to relocate to my new home, I had given up my office as a travel agent for the front desk as a receptionist but was expected to continue to sell vacations and be a receptionist as well. It was an impossible task on a good day – and most days weren't good ones.

I walked off the job and went to my new home to watch the trees grow. I had no idea what I wanted to do for the rest of my life.

A few days later I stopped to talk to my neighbor on my walk. He had just lost his employee at the taffy store he owned in Bodega Bay. That is how I came to my new career as a sales clerk selling saltwater taffy in a pink-and-white-striped candy store in Bodega Bay. It offered me a retreat and became my sanctuary. The window looked out at the Bay and Eureka Fisheries pier next door, giving me hours of entertainment while watching birds. And nobody comes into a candy store in a bad mood.

I watched red-necked phalaropes doing their whirling dervish behavior and marbled godwits drill for dinner. Short-billed dowitchers dabbled. Every day at the taffy store, I saw an osprey dive for fish. Black oystercatchers sometimes showed up near the shore and in my window view. Every day brought birds for me to watch, and sometimes in the thistle weeds in back of the shop, I could see rats competing with the finches for seeds.

One afternoon, I heard a commotion of squeaks and squabbles. I went to the window and looked out. Four young gulls were grappling for an unidentifiable object. Each had a corner of the odious object and were involved in an old-fashioned game of tug-of-war. A great blue heron stood on the sidelines, taking the role of a bored umpire. The noise had increased and soon attracted the attention of a brown pelican that sailed into the cove - like a big battleship sent into investigate. The gulls became extremely nervous as this big guy approached. Frantic to be the winner, each one continued to fight with vigor up to the very end.

The investigative pelican soon floated up to the group, causing the gulls to drop the object and retreat in haste. The pelican picked up the repulsive piece, tilted its head back appearing to swallow it, but instead, spit it out whole. Disgusted with these idiots that didn't know what real food was, the pelican sailed out of the cove. The gulls immediately resumed their game of tug-of-war. I got busy and never saw who won.

On another windy day at my window, I watched a ring-bill gull kiting over the Eureka Fisheries. The bird's attention was directed to what appeared to be a single pole antenna. Sure enough, he dipped a wing and made an attempt at the antenna. The wind blew him off course by a few inches, and he flapped his wings, made a circle and came back to the antenna. Again, he kited over the antenna, his head down in complete attention and after a few seconds, he dipped his wing and this time grabbed the tip of the antenna with his beak and pulled it upwards a couple of inches. He continued this game most of the day. Beam me up, ring-bill, I thought. On any windy day, I found him playing this game.

During the slow months, the taffy store brought me peace and pause for reflection. During the busy months the birds of Bodega Bay brought me laughter and joy, as I sold saltwater taffy by the sea.

A Bull Fight with a White Cape

Driving home from the taffy shop one evening at dusk, I saw a great egret fly into a field, probably for a snack before roosting. Just before landing, the bird spread its wings like a white parachute and for one brief second stood suspended in space before gracefully dropping to the ground.

Several cows grazed in the field nearby. One teenaged rambunctious bull decided this stranger from space had invaded his territory. He lowered his head, pawed the ground with a hoof, and charged the egret. Caught by surprise, the egret managed to pull up its wings and do a pirouette in the air just in time before landing further away. This act only angered the little bull even more. Once again, he put his head down and pawed the earth before charging. I almost imagined that I could hear the snort of hot air coming from his nostrils.

But this time, the egret was prepared to participate in the dance with the bull.

Gracefully extending its white cape of feathers in a seductive arc, it moved in a fluid movement upwards away from the bull before dropping the parachute downwards a few feet further away. The little bull, not to be deterred, charged once again. The graceful white cape flew up, proud and erect, ready to continue the bull -fight. There was no place to pull over and watch the finish of the bull fight with a white cape. The road curved and I lost sight of these two dancers dueling in the dusk.

A Thoughtless Tragedy

Chris Larsen, manager of Eureka Fisheries, brought my attention to two pairs of Western gulls that had built nests on the pier behind the taffy store.

One pair had nested on the left-hand side of the pier, and the other pair had built their nest in a hollowed out piling on the right side. I'm sure these were first-year breeding birds that had been pushed out of more favorable spots for nesting and found them settling for a less-than-desirable spot. The two proud parents I was able to watch outside my window sat patiently on the nest for weeks, guarding their precious three mottled brown eggs. Meanwhile, fishing season was in full force, and boats were pulling into the pier and unloading their catch directly beside both pairs of stressed but dauntless parents.

Finally, Chris came into the shop and announced the birth of two baby birds from the nest I had been watching from my window. For a couple of weeks, the parents took turns fishing to feed the voracious youngsters. Chris tried to keep the fishing people from disturbing the birds any more than was necessary and continued giving the birds bait.

Days turned into weeks, and Chris and I continued to have hope the two offspring might make it. Then one day, Chris came into the store to sadly inform me that one bird was missing. Two were there the night before he left work, and the next morning, only one was to be found.

A week later, the temperatures inland had soared to high numbers, and that weekend, tourists dressed in swimsuits with picnic gear and suntan cream began to swarm the coast for a reprieve. I happened to be working that weekend and noticed a group of people who had parked

17

directly behind the store next to the crab pots. I thought that seemed rather impudent at the time since it was private property but I got busy and forgot to see where they went.

Chris came into the store later that afternoon in an outrage. He had discovered this large family, complete with baby, kids, grandma, and a dog on the pier setting up to have a picnic. These thoughtless people had passed a sign saying "Keep Out", opened a gate bearing a "No Trespassing" sign, and made themselves as comfortable as if they were on a public beach.

Chris explained they had no business back there and asked them to leave. The mother immediately became rude and said, "We do it all the time."

Chris informed them, "Not anymore," and was pleasant enough to explain that he didn't want the liability of kids on the pier. The woman still didn't get it, and Chris finally said, "Let me explain it to you this way. How would you feel if I was to go to your house, walk through a gate with a sign on it saying "No Trespassing" and make myself at home in your backyard?" Grumbling, they finally departed.

Chris then discovered the other baby gull was missing.

We both stood there feeling a huge sense of loss and fury.

The insensitivity of one selfish family had wiped out the weeks of hard work and energy one pair of gulls had invested in trying to raise a family. Tragedy in nature happens every day.

But to have watched the building of a nest and observed the fragility of the eggs; to have watched the tenacious parents determined to stay on their eggs in the midst of chaos and the unloading of fishing boats, was, to Chris and me, like watching a small miracle happen.

In a world that seems to be filled with more and more disrespectful people, my righteous indignation made me realize why I preferred birds to human beings sometimes.

A Thoughtful Tragedy

After the loss of the two young gulls I had watched from the taffy store's window, I kept wondering when the other pair of gulls' eggs would hatch. They had built their nest approximately the same time as the other pair. Two weeks had now passed since the loss of the first gulls' babies.

The second pair of parents continued to sit patiently on their nest. I was beginning to think the eggs might be sterile. I was quite sure these were first-year breeding birds that had not been able to find a more suitable nesting site.

At last, I came to work wondering if the other two were still sitting on their nests. Chris Larsen came over as soon as he saw my car. One of the birds had hatched that night, he told me excitedly. Immediately I went with him to the pier to see the spectacle.

There was mother sitting on the nest, and she began squawking "gull ablatives" to us all. Finally she flew off the nest and landed just a few feet away. Sure enough, there in the nest was one mottled messed up baby bird, trying to stretch its wings.

But astonishing to both of us was the sight of another baby gull emerging from an egg. We withdrew from the close proximity of the nest. Mother immediately flew back to the nest, covering her treasures from the world.

Later that afternoon, Chris came into the taffy shop to tell me that a third egg had hatched, but the baby died halfway out of the egg. Even so, the odds seemed good, and we both had high hopes this family might have a better chance at survival than the first nesting pair.

The following week, I returned to the taffy store and immediately went to the pier to find Chris and get a report on the gulls. Chris and his partner met me with long faces.

Both baby gulls were gone. The day before, the chicks were in their nest, but when the men arrived at work that day, the chicks had disappeared. It didn't surprise me they didn't make it. The mortality rate for gull chicks is high, and I knew it.

We stood watching the gull parents calling and returning to the nest in distress. With a sinking heart, I looked at these two kind men, who had been their protector and friends. They had fed them bait, kept the fishing people from disturbing them when the boats came in, and shared with me the small miracle of watching a chick emerge from an egg. I had seen compassion and sensitivity from these two men.

Perhaps, the world wasn't so full of thoughtless people after all.

Small Efforts to Save a Bird

The weather was warm at the coast and infernally hot inland. Anyone lucky to have a day off headed for the coast. I was selling taffy and T-shirts as fast as I could bag and fold them. The season had peaked at Eureka Fisheries next door, and fishing boats were pulling up to the pier to unload their catches while trucks pulled into the dock to load and take them away.

Patient customers were lined up waiting to purchase their chosen bags of candy. The cash register was humming. In the midst of all the activity, I was surprised to see Chris Larsen trying to get my attention. "We have a sick cormorant flapping around over here," he said. "I'm too busy to do anything. Got any ideas?"

I nodded. "I'll call Wild Bird Rescue as soon as I can." Between ringing up taffy, I managed to get hold of a person on the phone that said they would try to find someone to come and get the bird.

About an hour later, Chris called me "One of the fishermen picked up the bird and pulled a large spiny object out of the cormorant's mouth," he said. "We fed it some fish, and it ate but it's still sitting on the pier in all this chaos and not looking well."

"I called Wild Bird Rescue and they are looking for someone to come pick up the bird," I answered.

A couple of hours later, Bill Evans from Wild Bird Rescue came into the shop and asked where the bird was. I directed him to the pier and asked him if he would come back and tell me what kind of a cormorant it was. He said he would be glad to.

A few minutes later, I was finishing up with a customer when Mr. Evans entered the store again called out "pelagic cormorant," then turned around and left.

I managed to stumble out after the customer and catch up to Mr. Evans. He had the sick, frightened bird in a box ready to take to the bird hospital. I gave Mr. Evans my card and asked him to keep me informed on the bird's recovery.

The next day, he called and reported the bird was still alive. It had been put on antibiotics but was quite underweight. And it had external and internal parasites. The next 24 hours would be critical.

Chris later explained to me that fishermen love cormorants. Cormorants have great fishing skills and for centuries have been exploited by man, especially in Asia, to fish for people. Chris also remarked how fragile the bird appeared except for his large legs and feet. To fish underwater at depths of more than 100 feet, cormorants need powerful webbed feet to propel themselves through the water.

The last report from Wild Bird Rescue was great news – the bird had returned to good health and would soon be released at Bodega Bay.

Thanks again to a caring fisherman, Chris Larsen, who stopped in the middle of work to bring the bird to my attention, and to Bill Evans, who picked up the bird and took it to Wild Bird Rescue. But the real heroes were at the bird hospital – the compassionate people who nursed the cormorant back to health.

Yes, some times the small things we do in life are worth the effort to help eliminate suffering and pain to our fellow creatures.

A Misplaced Visitor

One day, I looked out my window at the taffy store and saw a glimpse of what I first thought was a great blue heron but soon realized that it definitely was not. To my complete amazement, I realized it was a sandhill crane.

Now any self-respecting sandhill crane would not be found near the ocean. He would be making his wintering home inland and eating some farmer's harvested grain.

This lonely guy must have lost his way and decided to spend the winter out at Bodega Bay in the cove just behind my window. To my pleasure, this spot became one of his favorite places to hang out.

Sandhill cranes usually live on grain only, but this gutsy character learned how to hunt and eat a seafood diet. He used his long bill to fish and pluck morsels of food from seaweed. He watched and imitated the gulls – and sometimes, intimidated the gulls into giving up or sharing their dinner.

A few weeks later, I heard he was spending time down at the Tides on their pier, eating candy bars and other junk food that he begged from the tourists. Apparently, it was much easier for a misplaced bird to live on the streets, begging for a handout, than it was for a homeless person.

Eventually, the bird was trapped and taken to a Refuge Camp so he could be weaned off all the junk food and relearn a healthy sandhill crane diet, before being transported and released into a large sandhill crane flock.

I still wonder if it's possible to forget the taste of crab and candy bars after being introduced to these delicacies. I keep thinking that sandhill crane may take a detour while migrating one year and stop by Bodega Bay for another seafood dinner.

Living in Abundance

Chanslor Ranch at Bodega Bay was hosting a Festival, and Dennis and I were asked to lead a bird walk for about ten people. The morning was bright and beautiful with blue skies, and our walk through the wetlands and wild country was filled with many splendid birds in breeding plumage.

Returning from the walk, we joined a demonstration and found out how soft and cuddly bats can be. We also learned what Bodega Bay must have been like 14,000 years ago, with massive grizzly bears roaming the land and condors soaring above them in astonishing numbers.

The fog rolled in with a soft cool breeze, and we walked up the barren hills to a few cluster of stone outcrops. The cool fog circled around us as we listened to the Celtic music lilting upwards from the ranch. I felt my Irish genes begin to stir, taking me back to another time and place. But the wind rustled the California grasses, and I was brought back to reality and down to my knees with an excessive sneeze attack, complete with watery eyes and scratchy throat.

We had driven our new camper to Bodega Bay for our first shake-down run. The next morning I awoke to the sound of the waves and barking sea lions. The first bird song of the day was the sad plaintive flute-like song of the Swainson's thrush.

We began our day with a walk through the dunes. Calls of the white-crowned sparrows and California towhees punctuated with the soft cooing of the mourning doves greeting the day – a wild landscape setting unique to California. Red-winged blackbirds clung to the reeds in the marsh at the Rail Ponds singing their liquid melodious song of *konk-la-ree.*

A Eucalyptus tree grove seemed to be filled with the high-pitched lisping trills of cedar waxwings attracted by the enticing fragrant blooms. The birds flock together, their movements often unpredictable. The silky softness of their plumage appears to be painted on by a master artist.

Later we stood on Bodega Head looking through the telescope at a pair of pelagic cormorants perched precariously on a precipitous cliff, brooding eggs. A Western gull sat sleeping on a large messy nest, her feathers fluffed up against the blasting cold wind. Just below her, approximately ten feet away, a black-oystercatcher sat on an almost indiscernible scrap where she had laid her eggs.

At the Hole in the Head, a roost of black-crowned night herons, including young, preened their feathers in the warm morning sun while a barn swallow drifted and dipped several times for a drink of water.

As we headed back to the warmth of our camper, I felt grateful for enjoying a life full of abundance, including a new camper and a laptop computer. But I'm most grateful for living in Western Sonoma County where we call this beautiful place home.

Eating on the Wing

It was still dark and we were sleepy as we boarded the Tracer at Port O' Bodega Bay at 6:00 am. We were booked on a Shearwater Journey, one of Debra Shearwater's, pelagic birding trips to the Bodega Canyon and the Cordell Banks.

The Cordell Banks is located approximately 24 miles due west of Point Reyes. It is a shelf that drops off into very deep water. The currents hit this shelf and in turn bring the bottom water up to the surface along with an abundance of sea life, which attracts a profusion of bird and animal life.

I had not taken a pelagic trip in years. With the smell of the sea and the rocking of the boat as we set off, I felt the excitement of the unknown – anything is possible on one of these trips. All too soon I remembered the frustration of trying to hang on with one hand and focus the binoculars with the other one.

The first excitement of the day was sighting a great blue whale, largest of all animals in the world. I will never forget the sight of this magnificent animal breeching. Almost as if in slow motion, the immense creature rose out of the water and when the head went under, the body kept going and going and going until finally the tail appeared and then disappeared into the darkness of the water.

But the best was still to come.

Someone screamed, "Peregrine falcon carrying prey!"

I followed the pointing finger and carefully focused my binoculars on the falcon. It appeared to be carrying a large bird. The captive bird's tail feathers extended out past the tail of the falcon. Mesmerized,

I watched the falcon pluck off a wing and discard it like a drumstick. The white fragile wing splattered with blood floated gently down and landed next to the boat.

Someone yelled in astonishment, "It's a Bonaparte's gull!"

I looked up in time to see the other wing being severed and dropped. The falcon's head was turned downwards as it tore at the breast while flying.

Debra Shearwater's wild excitement was infectious. "The farthest out I've ever witnessed a peregrine falcon was eight miles!" Debra exclaimed – and we were 24 miles out at sea.

But there was more to come.

Five orcas – one male, one female, and three juveniles – were in a feeding frenzy. They had just killed a sea lion and were devouring it. We saw black and white markings brilliantly when they breeched. Suddenly, the carcass of the dead animal surfaced near my side of the boat. A red ball of bloody guts, lungs, and liver bobbed to the surface of the water.

The young orcas began to swim beside the boat, then dived down. In silent anticipation, we waited and watched as a white stomach surfaced and after a few seconds, disappeared again with the bloody mass.

We had witnessed the entire chain of a food cycle in the Pacific Ocean.

The currents brought krill, squid, and mackerel to the surface. Humpback whales ate the krill, and thousands of sooty shearwaters and gulls ate the krill and squid. Mackerel ate the krill and squid, and sea lions consumed the mackerel.

A family of orcas devoured the sea lion, and a peregrine falcon swooped down and grabbed a Bonaparte's gull, eating the gull on the fly.

Weary and filled with wonder at the inter-connectedness of life, we returned home.

Green Flashes and Dancing Ghosts

As I was driving home from the taffy store one Christmas Eve, I made a stop at Duncans Landing to watch the sunset. It was a spectacular evening with clear weather conditions and a full moon.

As I watched the red vibrant fireball melt into the deep blue ocean, I witnessed for the first time the phenomenon I had heard about but never seen – the green flash. The second the sun slipped out of sight below the water line, a green-blue light flashed from the center outwards. In a blink, it was gone.

I accepted this gift as a good omen for the coming year.

As I continued my drive home, a dark shadow suddenly came swooping down by the side of the road near Goat Rock Beach. It was quickly joined by a second dark shadow, and the two dissolved together into one. Clutching, grasping, and flapping the shadows appeared to be doing a death dance.

Stopping the car, I realized I was watching two great-horned owls in an elaborate mating dance.

Great-horned owls are among the earliest birds to breed in a year. Pair bonding often takes place in early winter. An unmated male will begin the ritual by choosing a proper nesting site. He will then begin dusk and dawn announcing his presence with heart-throbbing deep base booms. With any luck, a female will hear his promises and come closer to inspect his choice of real estate. If she finds him and his selection satisfactory, the couple will begin a long ritualistic sequence of mating events that eventually lead to copulation.

The ponderous, serious ceremony must be followed step by step.

It begins with a long-term duet of vocalizations. The male will call then pause, and the female answers. This will often go on for more than a month. As the climax nears the end, the calls become closer in intensity and eventually overlap, announcing the proof of the pair-bonding.

In addition to the vocalizations, the great-horned owls' mating behavior may include mutual grooming, ritual feeding, bill fending, and flamboyant dancing, such as I witnessed.

I will never forget that Christmas Eve – the sun's green flash as the sunset melted into the ocean, and the two great-horned owls like shadows suspended in air before disappearing over a ridge lit by a full moon.

Small miracles do happen at Christmas-time.

Goodbye to the Taffy Store

During our last trip, my husband said he didn't want to follow our usual schedule.

I explained that I had to be back in Bodega Bay for the taffy store, and he was not happy. We had a long discussion about the situation.

The end result is he wanted to travel more, and I wanted more time to write. My leisure time had almost disappeared in the active timber harvest battle we were fighting against the California Department of Forestry. I was delighted to find more writing assignments. But I was also finding less time for entertaining friends, bird watching, and gardening.

It was time for a change.

I remember gazing out the window at the bay on my last day. I reflected on all the special moments and dramas I had witnessed through that window.

The constant changing light on the water. The gorgeous sunsets and silhouettes. The eerie bird calls, the constant sound of flapping wings in the water, and the barking harbor seals as they swam gracefully by the window. The lonely sound of the foghorns at Bodega Bay. The smell of saltwater – and the fish smell of the Eureka Fisheries when it was a thriving business. Seagulls were always hanging out at the Eureka Fisheries then, as fish were unloaded. But now the Fishery was closed and stood empty as a ghostly pier. The gulls still circled overhead, probably out of habit. I remembered the many seagull scuffles I had observed.

I gazed out the window one last time, then turned on the alarm locking the door. I looked across the street at the meadow where I had watched deer and fox. A "For Sale" sign marked the empty, sagging pier that once was a place of activity. A housing development would soon take over.

All things change. And I knew I was making a timely exit.

The Redwoods

Mossy redwood trees

Dripping in the shadow green

Ancient ones weeping

Not in My Backyard

For 16 years I lived in Cazadero and never heard the sound of logging.

And then I began to hear it everywhere.

Each time I hear the thunderous roar through the forest of a redwood tree crashing to the ground, I know that not only has a tree just died but a small universe of inter-connected creatures have died too. Beetles, cicadas, insects, and hidden brown creeper nests to name a few have gone to their death with one redwood tree.

Birds and squirrels will have one less tree to harvest redwood cones and play among the branches. Logging trucks barrel down the narrow road next to my creek, chasing my dog and me to safety. I used to be able to hear the creek babble below my house, but recently on some days I only hear machines, back-up signals, the crash of redwoods, and the destruction of a creek where I once remember seeing salmon swimming upstream.

The controversial spotted owl has helped save a few forests from becoming a graveyard of stumps, marking the landscape like tombstones in memory of where they once stood. However, the battle over the spotted owl was taking place in some ancient forest somewhere in the Pacific Northwest, not in our backyard.

Another bird dependent on the continued existence of the redwoods is the marbled murrelet. It leaves the Pacific Ocean to nest in the coastal mountain range. Baby birds have fallen to their death when old trees have been logged.

Logging has always been a way of life and survival in these redwoods. I live in a house built of redwood. The redwoods in my neighborhood have been logged, burned over, and logged again by selective cutting. I don't oppose sensible selective cutting as it has been done in the past.

I do oppose accelerated clear-cut logging for greed – and I also believe we should be replacing every tree that goes down. Ancient redwood forests that stood at the time Christ was born should be able to stand until they fall on their own, and it is our duty to protect them at all costs.

Back in 1985, I flew over Oregon and Washington on my last flight as a flight attendant. Looking down, I saw a sea of green forests that appeared to go on forever.

Seven years later, my husband and I flew over the same area on a trip to Alaska. I stared out the window in absolute disbelief. No carpet of green was to be seen anymore. The ground appeared to be like a checker-board. Patches of clear-cut forests zig-zagged across the two states. The patches of green were fewer than the ugly scared patches of what use to be living forests. No place to hide the desecration from anyone up here, I thought. I turned cold with fury, tears streaming down my cheeks. How could this have happened in seven short years?

And it was then that my husband and I, and some close neighbor friends, started the long procedure to save 640 acres behind our homes from being logged. For five long years, we challenged the California Department of Forestry for approving three joined timber harvest plans. We raised money and hired a lawyer to sue the agency.

And we won our battle and went on to help organize other groups in Western Sonoma County to fight for their right to clean water and save their trees in their own neighborhoods.

Summer Magic

I threw a stick for Tory, my miniature poodle, on Austin Creek and he became a red blur of fur racing to retrieve it. At that moment I saw a movement out of the corner of my eye and immediately took in my breath and commanded, "Come, Tory." He bounded eagerly toward me, waving his tail, and I attached his leash. Fortunately, he hadn't seen what I had seen.

A female wood duck was hurrying her babies, who were getting much too close to where we were playing. My husband Dennis and I began to retreat further away so as not to disturb her. Twelve tiny bundles of down moved like wind-up toys. Mother took them to a large wood stump and hid them deep inside. Through our binoculars, Dennis and I watched them disappear into the darkness of the cavern. As we continued up the creek, mother duck decided it was safe to come out of the hiding spot, and we watched her lead her tiny fleet down to the creek.

As we continued our walk, a pair of chestnut-backed chickadees fed hungry babies who called and fluttered their wings to attract attention. Two yellow adult Wilson's warblers with black berets were being followed by hungry baby birds. A song sparrow with a dark badge on his streaked breast came down to the water's edge and plucked a juicy caterpillar in his beak.

We listened to the flute-like song of the Swainson's thrush who arrived a few weeks ago from their Southern winter grounds. Their call is one of the most haunting songs of summer and never fails to raise an emotional response in me. Though the call may be heard many times in the summer, the Swainson's thrush is secretive, and sometimes seldom seen. Always skulking along the bottom of the forest floors, it blends into the shadows, making it difficult to find. However, this one, unaware of us came out of the willows for a drink of water.

I heard quiet tapping and, looking up, found a juvenile downy woodpecker working on a narrow ash tree.

We cheered when an orange-crowned warbler appeared at the top of the willows and showed us its rusty orange cap before flying off.

We continued walking down the creek, admiring a green heron. Black phoebes flitted from one rock to the next. Robins bathed by the side of the creek while tree swallows, rough-winged and violet-green, swooped and sailed erratically in their pursuit of insects on the wing.

Suddenly, I saw a gray bird fly by me and it took a second for me to realize I had just seen a dipper, an extremely special bird. It landed about 20 feet away in a shallow area of the creek, where we watched it put its head under, grubbing for water bugs and other creatures.

This bird is usually easily found far up creek on King's Ridge Road. In over 30 years of birding our creek, we have seen the dipper only three times this far down the creek.

As we walked back up the road, we talked about the excitement of so many wonderful surprises in our own environment. The adventure of birding another destination always produces an adrenaline high. But it's nice to know we can continue to enjoy our birds at home with such enthusiasm.

Walking up the path to our house, we encountered another surprise. A small ring-neck snake squirmed off the trail and disappeared under a slash pile of natural debris. Its back was dark blue-green, and I could see the sides of its orange belly and its red necklace, which gives it the name. This too was another rare sighting as we have seen it as many times as we have the dipper.

There is always summer magic on our creek. All it takes to discover it is to be aware.

A Recipe for Love

I had set aside an entire day for writing. Dennis was gone and I had decided not to answer the phone or the door that day. After a few yoga stretches, I wandered out to the garden to check my flowers before heading upstairs to the computer. As I stood gazing at the roses, I noticed something near my feet.

It was a young black-headed grosbeak gasping for air.

Obvious to me, it was another window casualty. My heart sank. My writing day was being shot down by a bird.

I placed the grosbeak in a shoebox lined with a towel and gently checked it over. One eye was shut. The wings appeared to be okay, but the chick tended to lean in one direction. And it couldn't perch on my finger.

Probably a concussion, I thought. I checked the bird's craw and could tell it was empty. If it was going to survive, it needed to be fed, and neither parent was anywhere to be seen. I left the young grosbeak outside in the shade, hoping they would find it, and began searching for ingredients to make some baby food.

In the refrigerator I found some leftover white rice. One over-ripe banana I realized might be yummy with a bit of plum. Outside, I found wild strawberries. I'd seen them eat those before. *Whack* went the fly-swatter. A few flies for protein. Sorry, flies. I usually don't kill you, but this is an emergency. All the ingredients went into the blender along with some nonfat yogurt and milk. *Whirrr* went the blender.

Not bad, but a pinch of sugar might add some quick energy.

Holding my patient, I gently forced open its bill. Quickly I inserted the eye-dropper filled with the mixture. The bird eagerly swallowed my homemade concoction and immediately opened its mouth for another helping.

After its breakfast, I tried putting my finger out to see if it could perch. It tried several times unsuccessfully. The grosbeak needed rest, so I covered the chick with the towel and took it to my desk.

Every couple of hours, I stopped working and took the chick downstairs for feeding. Each time, the bird voraciously gobbled the mixture I had made.

Dennis returned in the evening and, after checking the bird over, agreed with my diagnosis about a concussion.

I continued the feeding through the night until we went to bed. The next morning, I had to go to work at the taffy store.

Dennis looked peeved as I gave the young grosbeak its first morning feeding, then handed the chick to him with instructions to continue its care and left for work.

But after my departure, Dennis decided to let his fingers do the walking through the yellow pages and called the Wildlife Care Center. They told him to take the bird to a veterinarian in Santa Rosa.

When Dennis arrived, he was asked to fill out a form and then was taken to the examination room. The veterinarian put the small bird on the huge steel table and with stethoscope and caring hands, began checking it over. He asked my husband what we had been feeding the chick. He said the bird was definitely well-fed, and he wanted my recipe. He confirmed our suspicions about a concussion. It might survive. It had a 50% chance of regaining its balance. It would be picked up by the Wildlife Care Center that day.

Neither my husband nor I ever called to find out if our bird had survived. We had become attached, and I preferred to think the youngster would be flying back to Mexico with the other black-headed grosbeaks this winter.

A Recipe Not Even for the Birds

About two weeks later, another juvenile black-headed grosbeak flew into a window.

It survived the crash, but was unable to fly. The bird let me pick him up without much reluctance, and I was sure that he was just momentarily stunned.

I placed him in the shoebox with a towel and kept an eye on him. I offered him some sunflower seeds, but he wasn't interested. Another hour went by, and I decided to start feeding him my concoction of rice, yogurt, banana, wild strawberries, and dead flies. This time, I added grapes instead of plums. I mixed it all together in the blender.

Smiling smugly to myself, I picked up the bird thinking how easy this was going to be since I had practice. I filled the eye dropper, gently forced the bird's beak open, then squirted food into its mouth.

The young grosbeak immediately shook its head in disgust and the food was dispersed in every direction but down its throat. Most of the concoction landed on me. I frowned but was now even more determined the bird was going to eat. Eventually, I managed to get some down its craw but not without a messy fight. The bird took water readily but obviously did not like my cooking. We went through this miserable process every two hours. By now, I was sure something was definitely wrong with the bird because I knew that it hated me so much, it would have flown away if it could.

My husband came home late that afternoon, and I described the scene. Dennis examined the grosbeak, then said, "There's nothing wrong with this bird."

40

"Then why won't he fly?" I asked.

Ignoring my question, Dennis put the bird on the ground. To my astonishment, the bird began hopping around, found a wild strawberry, and gobbled it down.

My self-confidence was shattered. You mean all this time I could have been feeding it strawberries and probably grapes too?

We watched the bird for several minutes as it hunted and ate strawberries, found a bug or two and gulped those down. It didn't fly but seemed quite capable of feeding itself. Eventually, the grosbeak disappeared into the darkness of the forest. I hope it was able to fly soon and not discovered by a predator.

The first one had just fledged and was still quite happy to be fed by its parents – in this case, me. The second one, two weeks later, was quite capable and happy to feed.

I prefer to think that it had nothing to do with my original recipe.

My husband and I have tried windsocks and black silhouette cut-outs of predators on most of our windows, but the birds continue to crash into them. We feel guilty enticing them into our yard by feeding them, only to find a few of them flying into our windows at break-neck speed.

Our window kills have included pine siskin, black-headed grosbeaks, one Wilson warbler, and a Pacific-slope flycatcher. The saddest loss was a MacGillivray's warbler. We have never seen one in our yard to count on our yard bird list before, and no, unfortunately, dead birds don't count.

Still, I'm amazed that more birds survive than die, and I have continued to save all survivors – even if they don't like my recipe.

The Monk in the Woods

My friend Heidi called me and asked if my weekend guest Ann and I would like to go with her to visit a Buddhist monastery in the woods behind Occidental. Heidi had met the monk in charge of Sunnataram Redwood Forest Monastery, and he had invited her to come any time.

After having visited Thailand and read the book *The Tibetan Book of Living and Dying*, I was intrigued and anxious to meet a real Buddhist monk.

Heidi joined Ann and me in Occidental. Directions in hand, the three of us followed a partially paved road leading to the top of the hill.

Draped in orange robes and smiling congenially, the monk stood waiting for us. I extended my hand and introduced myself. Placing his hand over his heart, the monk asked, "May I bless you with my heart?"

As we walked through the damp redwoods, Chutiko explained that his monastery belonged to the forest monks. He asked if and how we meditated. He told us there were many different forms of meditation. "When I lived in the forest of Indonesia, there were tigers, many dangerous snakes, and animals. Animals are peacefully drawn to the energy of meditation, and so I thought it wise to meditate 24 hours a day," he said.

His home was now a tiny hut with a small wood stove. His kitchen was outside under tarps. Like St. Francis Assisi, he lived alone with his meditations and the birds he feeds. We talked about the various birds he had seen there. Often a flock of wild turkeys came to roost in the tops of the redwood trees. Since he was close to the ocean, he had seen white pelicans fly over.

With the threat of rain, we began to walk through the monastery grounds. Many quiet corners had been turned into reflective places to stop and contemplate.

As we stood staring at vibrant green mossy branches, listening to the quiet breathing of the forest through what seemed a pale green veil, I heard the *chirrp chirrp* of the first varied thrushes to arrive on their wintering grounds.

We retreated to the *yerta*, a round communal building used for meditation. Chutiko told us he had studied most religions and they all had the same basic message. "In my hut, I have a picture of Buddha, Jesus Christ, my teacher, and a mirror, so I don't forget who I am," he laughed. Our visit ended with a meditation.

As Chutiko blessed us, he told us to keep our happy smiles because they meant a happy heart was inside. As soon as we pulled away in my car, it began to rain. My friend Ann said, "The rain knew to wait until we had completed our meditations and our visit." Indeed it did appear that way.

Meditation is the way I perceive most birds and animals to live their lives most of the time. They eat when they are hungry, lie down when they are tired, and sleep when they are sleepy. The rest of the time, they are peaceful and quiet with nature.

Our lives seem mostly full of distraction. I liked Chutiko, the gentle monk who lived in the woods in simplicity and silent reflection – like the animals and birds that surround him.

The Shortest Day of the Year

As I wondered why I never seemed to get much done these past days, I was suddenly reminded that the shortest day of the year was sneaking up on me.

These winter mornings of darkness made me want to crawl deeper under the covers and snooze away the morning. Instead of rising at 6:30 am as usual, I found myself sleeping later and later. In the afternoon about the time I was involved in a writing project, I was aware of it getting darker.

Living in the redwoods during these intermittent drizzles slows down most of us rain lovers. This is the time to reflect, read books, bake cookies, or just sit and ponder. I love the occasional rays of light coming through the smoke from our neighbors' wood stoves.

As I stood at the kitchen sink watching the rain come down, I also enjoyed the dark-eyed juncos scampering below our feeder. The flock could seem invisible in the darkness and shadows of the dismal days. Only the flickering of their white tail feathers, flashing like lightening bugs, made me aware of their movements.

There is something comforting in the mourning doves' silhouettes, sitting on our split rail fence all fluffed up, ignoring the rain. They were my year-round sentinels, reminding me they will still be here in the spring, and the spring would return.

Winter also brings one of our prettiest visitors to our yard – the varied thrush. Its only utterance a low *chhrrrkk*, this quiet bird of the deep forest sports a black necklace on an orange breast and a bright orange stripe above its eye. The thrushes winter over in our forests before returning to breeding grounds as far north as Alaska.

With the shortest day of the year, December 21st, almost upon us, I couldn't help but think how glad I was to be departing in January for the warmer weather of Costa Rica and Honduras. When my husband Dennis and I return one month later, suntanned and relaxed, daffodils will be blessing us with their sunshine blush of warmth even through the continuing rain. The coast will begin to have days of blue sky, white puffy clouds, and blowing winds.

The swelling Austin Creek in March and April would beckon us to try a fast ride to the river in our kayak. I would begin to watch for the wood ducks and common mergansers pairing up in preparation for the hard work ahead of raising another family.

My hyacinths, freesias, and tulips would begin to unfold their soft petals to the warmer days, displaying an abundance of color to celebrate the coming of spring. And in April, I will be on the look out for the first fuzz of the pussy willows to pop out, promising the emergence of green leaves.

May would remind me to watch for the shadows of water bugs appearing on the quieter shallows of Austin Creek. The rhododendrons will be in full bloom, and I would begin to watch for pregnant white-tailed does giving birth to spotted fawns with unsteady legs.

And with the insects, our spring migrants would soon return to usher in spring at its fullest.

A Killer Instinct

My potting shed had become a mildewed, mice infested mess. It was time to paint the inside – a task I found to be therapeutic and meditative.

My husband built my shed with glass windows so I could watch the birds come to the feeder. The only sounds I could hear were the birds fluttering close by and the cracking of sunflower seeds, along with the scratching of the towhees on the ground beneath the feeder. *Thump, thump, thump,* went a squirrel across the top of the shed. I poked my head out the door and peered upwards. The squirrel pounced for the nearest tree limb, scolding me with a *chkkk chkkk chkkk chkkk.*

My neck began to ache, and it was time to take a break for lunch. As I walked to the door of the house, I looked down and my eyes focused on a bird lying on the ground. I reached down and picked it up.

It was a juvenile junco, another window fatality. The broken bird was just beginning to become stiff. I stroked the soft feathers and cradled its still warm body in my hand. Finally, with a sad heart, I placed the dead bird on the deck railing and went inside.

A few minutes later, I returned to the sliding glass door, preparing to go outside and continue my project. I came to a standstill immediately, placing my hand down with finger pointed to warn my dog to halt.

A Stellar's jay had landed on the rail of the deck. His attention was centered on the dead junco. His body posture was erect with excitement. With three quick hops, he perched next to the bird, staring intently with beady eyes. I was riveted to my spot by the door. But nothing prepared me for what I witnessed in the next few seconds.

The jay's sharp bill came down four quick times with deadly accuracy on the back of the junco. *Zing, zing, zing, zing,* just like in Hitchcock's movie, *Psycho.* There was no mercy.

I had definitely witnessed a cold-blooded murder – but the victim, unknown to the jay, was already dead. The jay then picked up his fresh trophy and flew away with it, disappearing through the trees.

I stood frozen with disbelief. First of all, jays do not eat carrion. And second, I was shocked by the violence of what I had seen. Jays will eat the young of small birds, and I believe this particular jay thought the junco was alive.

Walking back to my shed, I thought about how this unlucky baby junco had become an accident window fatality and within one or two hours became the food for a baby jay that will mature, fly, and mate to continue the circle of life.

Is it Endangered?

$\mathcal{A}$s I walked under the tall canopy of spires in the gothic redwood forest, I felt the magic of this sacred place as I saw it through the eyes of our four year old grandson, Taylor.

Trees surged high above us, seeming higher than buildings. Gnarled and knotted limbs distorted with age and beauty somehow seemed graceful, while green velvet moss carpeted dead trees rotting on the ground. Rays of sunlight captured dust particles that appeared to be spotlights in the dark green forest.

Taylor held my hand tightly as we hiked through the shadowy forest headed for the creek. The muffled silence matched the odor of the earth dampness.

The day was a warm Indian summer day with riots of reds, oranges, and yellows contrasting with the green forest. Usually Austin Creek is a small stream of puddles at this time of year. But due to the early rains we had in September, the creek was much wider and running clear.

I watched Taylor throw stones in the creek and giggle as we watched, our 16-year-old poodle, chase the splashes the rocks made. We found steelhead fingerlings in the shadows near the rocks. We captured yellow-legged frogs jumping in the creek bed, and I watched Taylor's face become serious when his father handed him one and instructed him to hold it gently. Wide-eyed and innocent, Taylor looked up at me and asked, "Is it endangered?"

Extinction has been a part of evolution from the beginning. But Taylor's question provoked me to ponder how the word "endangered" came to be and why a four-year-old is already aware that his world is not a safe one.

Endangered is definitely a modern concept developed by our culture. Since 1600 to 1975, the rate of extinction of bird and mammal species was estimated to be fifty times higher than what it took eons of time. Nature has lost its innocence and the parade of endangered species can't be replaced.

The spotted owl represents to me the pending death of my land, my home. Most people wouldn't know a spotted owl if they saw one. I'm a bird watcher. I live in the redwoods. I travel and I camp and I still have not seen one.

As little as 5 to 10% of the original old growth forests are left in the Pacific Northwest. This fragile owl was able to stop the chainsaws, sparing many redwood trees as it became the mascot for controversy, contempt and conflict.

I understand what motivates the rednecks and loggers who find it congenial to shoot or assault wildlife and wilderness. They are the last of the mountain men, the cowboys to prevail. They are fearful and powerless and know that life on their terms is coming to an end, and, through fear and anger have found it easier to pick up a gun or chainsaw and assault the wilderness they deeply love.

Our wildlife managers have continued the assault politically by implying a superiority over nature with a need to control and manage. I'm sure their intentions were good; however, this philosophy has driven us to the edge.

The struggle goes on. The powerful willing and able to strip a forest and cause the extinction of not just an owl, but an entire ecosystem. The less powerful, our children, willing to gather peacefully to protect all that is good, even when taunted by those in power.

As I watched our grandson exploring a world of beauty that might be gone in his lifetime, I know that whatever we do to nature, we are only doing to ourselves.

Coming in for the Kill

A neighbor stopped by the other day and as we chatted outside on the porch, I heard a high-pitched death squeal of alarm.

A shadow descended like a dark cape, and the predator then came into view. A red-shouldered hawk plummeted from the sky with talons ready for the kill. He landed on the side of a large fir tree approximately ten feet away from us. He missed by a fraction of an inch, and a terrified chickaree scampered to safety.

The hawk hung suspended with his 45-inch wingspan spread to the maximum. His black and white feathered cloak appeared as ominous as if he were dressed to do battle. Hanging on to the side of the tree like a woodpecker was hardly a dignified posture for a hawk, and he soon let go and flew up to a branch to recover from his miss. Putting a bill to a ruffled feather, he smoothed his wings in quiet composure. Silently he glided down through the dense trees and disappeared from sight.

The drama was over in a few seconds, and my neighbor sadly missed the entire scene. This scene occurs daily but is rarely captured by humans. I wondered later if we had distracted him the last second and that was why he missed his target.

Red-shouldered hawks live in wet lowland coniferous forests near creeks. They are one of the prettiest of North America's hawks, sporting a bright orange belly and rufous patches on each shoulder that are not always visible. They are vocal in the spring and can be heard repeating rapidly, "kee-you, kee-you, kee-you." Stellar's jays know how to mimic the call perfectly.

I have seen red-shouldered hawks perched on wires almost every time I have driven out to Bodega Bay. However, the Sonoma County Breeding Bird Atlas field studies showed little evidence of breeding red-shouldered hawks at the coast and northwestern interior of Sonoma County.

We have a bird-feeding station that sits just six feet from the tree where this incident happened. Squirrels, chickarees, and many birds frequent it during the day.

After this particular incident, the feeding station sat quiet and empty for the rest of the day.

They're All Good Birds

Saying goodbye to our fellow birding group at Duncans Mills, one member said, "It's too bad there weren't any good birds today."

That thought stayed with me as we drove home. Truth spoken, there weren't any rare migrants or unusual birds seen that day. It was still early in the season.

The warm Indian summer day was filled with fall color and clear blue sky. We had started the morning wearing fleece, and by 10 am we were taking it off.

The first birds of the day were a flock of wild turkeys in the fields next to Duncans Mills. We parked the car next to the eucalyptus trees and watched 46 California quail pecking in the dark shadows near the old schoolhouse. A Nuttall's woodpecker kept making a rolling *prrrt* call that kept us looking upwards in hopes of locating it. One single bluebird sat in the sun on the wire, showing off its rusty pink breast and stunning blue feathered back.

Pygmy nuthatches sang their pandemonium of high-pitched twittering *pip, pip, pip, pip, pip,* over and over. All the birds were there just as they should be, doing what they are supposed to do. That is, with the exception of the migrants we hoped to see passing through.

We crossed the street to bird the willows and river from the bridge. A double-breasted cormorant stood on a rock in the river with its wings spread, soaking up the warmth of the sun. White gulls flew overhead against blue sky.

A Cooper's hawk swept by fast, disappearing behind the trees and out of view. A few late-migrating tree swallows darted back and forth over the water. Both least and western sandpipers chased after small animal life near the river's edge. Further down the river, a pair of killdeer stood and occasionally sprinted near the water.

The group strolled down toward the Bed and Breakfast Inn and we were rewarded with a good view of a female western tanager who was feeding in the shadows of a purple ornamental plum tree that had grown up wild through a berry bush. She was a greenish-yellow with dark wings and knowing these birds are prone to wander, I wondered where she had been.

A spotted towhee emerged from the bushes, but stayed close to the shadows, scratching in the dirt. We all stopped to admire the Inn's garden of fall blooms, where a pipe vine swallowtail perched on a blue morning glory – a black swallowtail edged in white teardrops with wings spread on a baby blue flower.

A monarch butterfly rested on the side of an orange dinner plate dahlia, its intricate black etchings appeared like a stained glass design. A sharp-shinned hawk swooped high above our heads.

The group wandered down to the campground, heading for the river's edge. A mew gull slept on a small island, sharing it with several peeps including a spotted sandpiper that dipped its rump up and down. Band-tailed pigeons flew across the river landing in the tops of trees. An immature black-crowned night heron flew into view and landed on a branch.

We enjoyed lunch in the sun behind the museum at Jenner. The smell of the salty air mixed with sandwiches and fruit. We watched egrets flapping their wings like white sheets, while pelagic and Brandt's cormorants streaked low over the water. After lunch, we drove over to Willow Creek Road in hopes of finding raptors. But with the sun high in the sky, the birds had all had their lunches, too, and were now taking siestas.

And so the group dispersed, and that brings me back to the beginning.

Roger Tory Peterson always hated to hear someone ask him, "Have you seen any good birds lately?" To him, all the birds were good.

I remember as a beginner birder, I would go on a bird walk and always bring home the memory of a new bird I'd seen. Eventually, the days came when I began to be disappointed because I hadn't seen anything new.

Now, I go with the group to enjoy the camaraderie, not expecting to see anything new and am pleased when I do.

After returning home from the walk, I perched myself on the chaise lounge with a glass of ice coffee and a book. Suddenly I looked up and saw a young male black-headed grosbeak fly to the bird bath. This grosbeak should have left for his southern wintering grounds about a month ago. Did this one get left behind or is he traveling from farther north, I wondered. He was certainly thirsty as I watched him dip his bill and drink more than 20 times. This was my unusual sighting for the day.

They're all good birds.

A Rare and Rosy Regale

As I looked out the kitchen window, my heart started thumping with excitement.

There at the bird feeder was a rose-breasted grosbeak.

Dennis came in the back door and I shouted for him to come quickly. After confirming what I'd seen, we both did a little dance at the kitchen window.

The rose-breasted grosbeak is the eastern counterpart to our western black-headed grosbeak. A stunning bird, he was dominating the bird feeder. Several female and juvenile black-headed grosbeaks and two males were attempting to perch on the feeder. The rose-breasted grosbeak refused to relinquish his new treasure trove.

Having made a wrong turn at the Sierras, he hadn't found a mate, and his hormones were still raging. The black-headed grosbeaks had already successfully completed their first brood and were feeding young. Their hormones were no match for this new visitor.

We made a telephone call to our neighbor and fellow birder, and she came down immediately to see him. Sitting at the kitchen island, we ate lunch and admired him with many "oohs and ahhs."

A couple hours later, I was upstairs working at my computer when I heard the loud thump of something hitting the window. I jumped up and looked out. There was the rose-breasted grosbeak on top of my carport on its back, convulsing in the throes of death – or so I thought.

I let out a scream.

We get our first rare bird in a year and it flies into the window and kills itself. Dennis came running into the room to see what had happened. Tears streaming down my face, I pointed at the window and told him to look down. The rose-breasted grosbeak was now on its belly. Dennis looked at me appalled.

Downstairs, Dennis got the ladder, crawled up, and retrieved the bird. The grosbeak was able to perch on Dennis' finger for a few seconds.

We checked him over. His bill, wings, and eyes seemed to be okay. He blinked blearily and closed his inner eyelid. I ran for a box and a towel; we placed him in the partial sunlight to keep him warm. We had done all we could for him. We assumed he had knocked himself silly, possibly giving himself a concussion. Now, only time would tell.

About an hour later, I realized I had better leave soon if I wanted to take him to Bird Rescue before they closed. I came downstairs with my keys and purse in hand. Dennis went over to take a look at the bird when suddenly the bird flew up into a tree and sat. He'd saved me the trip.

Even though we were glad the grosbeak could fly, we were still concerned. Many birds that hit windows will recover, only to fly off and die of a concussion somewhere else.

We rested easier when we saw him return that night and eat at the bird feeder.

We rejoiced the next morning when we saw that he had made it through the night and was eating with a strong appetite.

These birds usually show up on the western front in early spring. They are rare but regular. Since this was the middle of June, we have no idea where he came from or which direction he was going. Dennis thought that perhaps he would stay the rest of summer and go south again with the black-headed grosbeaks. It might help save his life if he did. He was with us for one week before disappearing.

Safe journey, little friend.

Writing for the Trees

The flyer came in the mail.

It simply stated that I was invited to a writing retreat for women. It would be held at the Sacred Grove Women's Forest Sanctuary near Garberville and we would be **WRITING FOR THE TREES.**

Since I'd been writing letters to oppose a couple of timber harvest plans that could occur on Austin Creek, this sounded tempting. Writing letters to the California Department of Forestry is hardly creative writing. Although the tactics derived to sabotage a timber harvest plan must be creative, the writing is mostly tedious.

I checked the date on the flyer, and the weekend was clear. I had been hoping something like this would come my way, and I mailed my check and started packing the car with tent, sleeping bag, camping gear, and a new journal and pen.

Listening to Glenn Yarbrough and Joan Baez in my tape deck, I sailed northward through the trees. This was going to be a whole new experience for me, as I had never participated in a writing retreat or a women's group.

My first task at the Sanctuary was to find a good flat spot for the tent and see if I was still a good girl scout who could erect a tent.

The other women began to arrive – eight earthy baby boomers, each powerful in her individual endeavors.

The Sacred Grove Women's Forest Sanctuary consisted of 14 acres of big trees along the Mattole River. The vision of the four women who bought the Sacred Grove was to protect the land as an act of healing and reconciliation with nature and to create a space of sanctuary where women and their allies could hear the wisdom of the ancient forest.

The opening ceremony was celebrated beneath two ancient redwood trees larger than any I had ever seen in Armstrong Woods.

Later at dinner, we were told the story of how this grove of trees was rescued from the loggers of the past. The wife of the man who owned the land insisted that she have some trees facing her house so she could see the trees and take walks in her forest. I would imagine that she and her husband had a few late night discussions before her stubbornness won the battle.

For two days we meditated, chanted, and wrote. Our writing assignments were guided and often it seemed like we were writing in trance. I had never experienced anything like it before.

The Aborigines know of the power of trance and meditation through their walkabouts. The native people of the Americas had rituals steeped in their trances and dream world. The power of writing in this state is in the opening of creative channels.

However, in opening those channels up, I experienced a strong opening up of myself emotionally. And sometimes, the writing became terribly sad.

In one of our exercises, we were to take a walk and find something to focus on and ask it for some wisdom. I came upon a pile of feathers.

A Pile of Feathers

A pile of gray feathers soft as down was mixed with redwood needles. I sat quietly and bowing with my hands clasped offered a prayer. Safe journey, little friend.

Picking up one of the feathers, I asked gently, "Who were you?" The answer came fast.

"I was a mourning dove who came to rest between the giant trees."

"And what happened to you," I asked, "that brought you to a pile of feathers instead of the soft living bird that sings the sad mournful song?"

"I was embraced by a Northern spotted owl that was hungry and began his search for dinner early while I rested in the last dapple of sunlight," came the answer.

"And how did that feel?" I asked.

"At first I was terrified, but that soon gave way to a quiet shock as the blood began to flow from my broken neck and mixed with the smell of death. And then I felt love that was as sweet as my mournful song.

"And I knew why I finally sang my song while I was alive. The love was for the young owlets who fed on my body so they could survive to hear the sad sweet call that my babies will sing to them."

Later that afternoon, we sat next to the Mattole River, writing Haiku. Japanese haiku consists of 3 lines. Its simplicity and structure make it excruciating and painful to learn and do well:

> Hey, squirrel in high canopy –
> What you say you fall from tree?
> Squirrel says catch something fast.

On Sunday after the closing ceremony, lunch, and goodbyes, I sailed home, but this time I had Freedom Rock songs from the 60s blasting loud from my tape deck. I felt wild, free, and open.

Writing for the Trees was one exciting and wonderful weekend.

Keeping the Wild Alive

On December 20th, 2001, our neighborhood was given the best Christmas present ever.

Austin Creek Alliance (ACA) won their court case against the California Department of Forestry (CDF). The judge ruled against the filing of the Timber Harvest Plan (THP) – and ruled for us on every single count stating that "the CDF had shown prejudicial abuse of its power."

After three long years, this was a great success for ACA.

The group included an artist, a writer, a lawyer, an art professor, a math professor, two teachers, a horse show producer, a student, a nurse, and retired elders, among approximately 100 other individuals. Together they learned how to read and shred THPs, hired their own geologist to give them a report and organized email and phone lists.

Another part-time neighbor, a lawyer who found the notice about the logging stuffed in his mailbox, came to ACA's aid – Environmental Law Foundation matched every dollar of contributions in the year 2000.

ACA was able to raise $14,000 for court costs.

When one person was busy or away, another person willingly stepped in and took over. Never did anyone's ego overstep another's.

Winning this case, of course, didn't mean the landowner would not file another plan. But two years of better environmental rules regarding THPs had come in place since then. The owner would have to follow the new rules and, of course, ACA would be there at the CDF table to see that the plan would be done according to the Forest Practice Rules.

These are some of the unsung heroes of today trying to make a difference in their own backyard all over the country. They are the writers who struggle to instill a love of the world around them with their words. They are the photographers who catch a perfect moment in time for us to witness. They are the artists who through their visions have created pictures to inspire us. They are politicians and lawyers who are trying to help save our planet. They are the tree huggers who bring attention to the cause.

But most often, they are good citizens who have made a difference in some small way by donating money or time. The environmental lawyers need the tree huggers to get the word out. No one is more important than another.

We can only begin to make a difference if we respect each other's voice in the cause.

Kohute Creek is a far cry from the Grand Canyon, but the endangered fish resting in the pools of the creek during summer are every bit as important. The members of ACA will enjoy knowing the fish will continue to survive in pristine water instead of choking to death after a logging operation had polluted 15 streams, crossing with heavy equipment – pollution that would have followed with the approval and stamp of the CDF.

I feel blessed to live in a strong community. I feel safer knowing these good people are my neighbors. I know I trust and respect them. By their involvement and passion, they made a small difference to keep the wild alive.

Faced with three adjoining THPs coming up for approval by the CDF with a cumulative impact of 645 acres adjacent to our homes, our neighbors called a meeting on a Sunday afternoon and asked the question, "What can we do?"

Thanks to my wonderful neighbors, I know I will never ask that question again. The answer is "a lot!"

A Walk on Dry Austin Creek

A burst of heavy wing beats exploded above our heads as a flock of approximately 60 band-tailed pigeons took to the air, causing my heart to race with surprise.

Black silhouettes against blue sky made me wonder what it must have been like to see darkness suddenly when thousands of passenger pigeons blurred the sky, erasing the light of day.

As we continued our walk, my husband Dennis and I felt sadness mix with our bittersweet success when Austin Creek Alliance won our logging case a few years back. The gates were open to the property and big machinery was in place as we heard the first chainsaws roaring.

We had spent many days at the California Department of Forestry (CDF), making certain the CDF did follow the Forest Practice Rules while the owner's Registered Professional Forester negotiated a new plan. The plan was finally approved and the logging was to begin.

I hurried past the property, not wanting to hear the felling of the trees as their limbs and bodies came crashing down – ending their lives as well as the creatures dependent on the trees. At least it wouldn't be happening in the springtime when the birds began their nesting season.

To distract ourselves, we decided to take a walk on the creek. The creek bed was chalky white with only a few holes and puddles of water left. The trees had a twinge of fall colors.

A great blue heron stood tall and erect next to a puddle, hoping a fish would come out of hiding under the rocks. His feathered cloak shone like blue steel, and his yellow bill was the color of sunflowers in the sunlight. He lifted his cape and rose in the air, gliding upstream to the next puddle.

I saw a movement close by. I couldn't believe my eyes. A river otter covered in mud stood just 10 feet from me. My dog Tory saw it too, and I tightened his leash as we watched it slide up some rocks to the creek's bank to hide. In these small puddles, what few fish and crawfish are left make an easy meal for the river otters, egrets, and herons.

A small flock of foraging chestnut-backed chickadees flew to the high branches of willows, followed by a large flock of bush-tits who were busily gobbling insects for breakfast.

I caught a glimpse of yellow and, focusing my binoculars on the movement, saw my first Townsend's warbler of the fall emerge. She was greenish on the back but yellow on the belly and had a grayish cheek spot. She will stay here now through the winter.

I kept hearing a one note cheep behind me and turned to see if I could find what was making the sound. At the foot of a gray blue willow beside a large pool, I saw movement. A small olive-brown bird turned around and I gasped when I saw her bright yellow throat. It was the first common yellowthroat we had ever seen on the creek in over 20 years. Once found by water on almost every outing, this beauty is not so common anymore and is thought to be in trouble as its numbers keep falling.

Chickadees dipped and sipped fluttering over the water. Another Townsend's warbler travelled with them, a brilliant yellow male with a black head, throat, and cheek patch.

Acting like a woodpecker, a tiny brown creeper worked on the end of a dead stump. A great egret flew past us, her wings flapping like starched white sheets in the wind. She landed beside a puddle and began her patient wait for a fish to come by. Two mallard ducks shared the same puddle.

A green heron landed in the branches overhead. The sunlight bathed him in glossy blue green on his back showing off his deep chestnut neck and face and shaggy crest.

One of the largest puddles had 16 ducks cavorting together. Most of them were mallards, but four immature or female common mergansers spooked and took to the air, showing big white patches on their wings. As we ended our walk, I put my hand out to stop Dennis from moving forward. I pointed to a wire about 25 feet away.

A red-shouldered hawk was perched on the wire, overlooking the creek. His reddish-brown wings and breast matched the color of falling redwood needles. His wide tail had bold black bands on both sides. Suddenly, he took off silently, showing the speckled flecking below his rufous shoulders, and we were able to see the crystal windows near his wrists.

This was the perfect ending to our walk on dry Austin Creek, and I hadn't even thought about the logging once.

A Stormy Christmas Season

Stumbling down the steps after the raging storm that night, I opened the door and stood there in dismay.

Perched on the hood of my husband's truck was a huge 10-inch-in-diameter tree branch.

Other branches had struck blows to our favorite hazelnut tree. I had to fight my way through the wet branches to get outdoors and retrieve the newspaper. Outside, I could see the gate had been damaged, and another huge branch hung precariously on the top of the house over my car.

Living under the trees, we've sat out many storms but this first storm of the year – with 50 mph winds – was a doozy, and we would be hit by many more, lined up in sets like waves.

As we began a third day without power, the phone continued to ring when neighbors discovered we were now without water. Dennis is always Mr. Fix-it and I'm always the one who gets involved when it comes to fighting timber harvest plans or getting rid of bad dogs running loose in our neighborhood. But sometimes there isn't an easy way to fix it other than to tell them to save rain water to flush toilets.

Standing at the kitchen sink, I watched a chickaree sit in the rain, voraciously eating black sunflower seeds at our bird feeder. His tail was tucked over his head like an umbrella.

A dark fox sparrow appeared at the base of the feeder almost like a shadow as it scratched for seeds. Gray squirrels scurried across a redwood tree, leaping from one wet branch to another.

Three varied thrushes with their bold necklaces appeared cryptic in color, almost fading into the dark underground. A flock of ten chickadees took turns at the feeder, sharing the suet block we had hung from the hazelnut tree that sparkled with tiny raindrops – unlike my Christmas tree inside covered in bird ornaments but no lights due to the power outage.

Two hummingbirds continued to chase each other as they had for the past two days. How do these animals and birds survive the storms, I wondered?

The day before, gales of wind raced through the tops of the redwoods, causing them to swirl with such force I cringed watching them. Dennis and I had witnessed two branches bringing down several other limbs as they crashed to the ground. Their ends came down like spears.

I wondered if the squirrels and chickarees had been terrorized while holding on with all their might to the swirling tree – and how many had fallen to their death when their branches gave way to nature's pruning.

As I pondered these thoughts, a moth fluttered by the window in random flight. Where had this fragile creature found refuge from the night? Where did the hummingbirds sleep while the winds howled and the torrential rain came down? Did the storm cause them fear as it did in me?

But while I stood watching them, it was apparent that all was normal now in the pursuit of food and in filling their small niche in the world. When our comforts are taken away, depression, cabin fever, and anger takes the edge, unlike the animals and birds, who seem to continue the cycle of survival in a complacent accepting manner of "here it is again – just another day."

And so this year, after seven days of no power to our community, my Christmas tree has become the hazelnut tree as I seem to watch it more than one inside with no lights. Its bare branches have become the arms that hold our feathered friends, its sparkling droplets twinkling like Christmas lights.

Moments Never Forgotten

If the sky could shine

It would reflect the color

Of mountain bluebirds

The Case of the California Condor

Thirty-eight years ago while living in Southern California, I took an ornithology course from Arnold Small to study the birds of California. On a field trip with the class, I saw my first and only California condor.

We had been birding all day with no luck. It was in the late afternoon on top of Mt. Pinos when most of us were involved with our barbecues and cookout preparations.

Arnold Small suddenly yelled out in excitement.

Fortunately, I was still wearing my binoculars and looked up just in time to see a gigantic bird soar low overhead, like an early flying reptilian dinosaur. Its shadow shared ours briefly before it disappeared. I was one of the few who even saw it.

Once, the California condor ranged over most of western North America, from Canada and into Baja California. The ranch lands north of Los Angeles may have looked ideal, but instead became the last stand for the survival of the condor. In fact, this territory was terrible habitat full of man-made dangers to the birds. Power lines and airplanes brought many of the birds crashing to the ground, while lead bullets in deer and cyanide baits for coyotes poisoned the birds when they ate the toxic carrion. Ignorant hunters took pot shots at the condors helping to decimate the few numbers left of this magnificent bird species.

The condors' plight soon became a social test case. Eco-systems became ego-systems, and the desperation of "what to do about the condors" exploded out of helpless frustration and madness. The California condor had become a symbol of our culture, representing our efforts on behalf of all endangered species.

Many ecologists believed that taking the condors out of the wild and restricting them to zoos was not to save them, but in fact, to lose them.

The scientists' goal was to offer a captive breeding program to manage maximum reproduction and genetic diversity with the end result to release and reintroduce chicks back into the wild.

On Easter Sunday, 1987, silence filled boardrooms, offices, and scientific labs. The last condor in the wild was captured and transferred to a zoo. The total captive population of birds was 27.

In the last desperate minutes to save the condor, bureaucrats and biologists continued to bull each other, while poetic ecologists waited to hear the last whispers in the wind as the condor took its final flight in the wild.

With all the rumbles and trembles that took place as egos clashed, is it any wonder that the final resting place of the wild condors was located over the San Andreas Fault? Did we lose touch with the condor as a wild creature when it was locked away in a zoo? Did our symbol of endangered species become demystified when we made it a laboratory experience? Or have we through science, genetics, and reintroduction saved the wild California condor from extinction? These were the questions we were asking ourselves at that time.

I believe that through science, we were able to make an all-out last ditch effort to save the condor, and in the end numbers most certainly make the recovery look successful. But something in me aches that we had to let it come to this point. What has happened in the history of the California condor in the twentieth century is an example of what is happening with other endangered species.

The focus has been on controlling nature, concentrating on identifying single problems for single species, and generating solutions with bio-power. And we have accomplished this with some success.

However, if we can't construct a more global, universal way of approaching all our species in a revolution of awareness and consciousness without the need to focus in the last desperate moments on single species, I fear our own survival may be at stake.

A Rare Encounter

Thirty some years ago on a Christmas Bird Count at Lake Lagunitas in Marin County, California, my husband and I witnessed something special that I have never forgotten.

It was a freezing cold day where we were birding the lake edge. As we came out of the trees and into a clearing, we noticed a deer standing stock-still in the bright sunlight, approximately 65 feet away from us. To our amazement, we observed a scrub jay fly over to the deer and land on its back.

We watched in wonder as the jay began a deliberate, meticulous task of what appeared to be grooming the deer, working its way up the deer's back towards the head. The doe stood dead still, her head up, a benign expression of pleasure on her face. She reminded me of my dog when I scratch her chest.

The scrub jay continued its way down between the ears, cautiously grooming the forehead, between the eyes. The process lasted about five minutes, and we assumed the jay was harvesting ticks.

For years I've asked other bird watchers in my area if they had ever witnessed any behavior like this. Most of them looked at me doubtfully when I explained what we saw. It was an unsolved mystery – until I got in touch with Cornell University.

Eventually, I sent an e-mail message to Cornell University, asking if anything had been published regarding a symbiotic relationship between these two species. By that evening, I had received an e-mail from John Fitzpatrick, Director of the Cornell Lab of Ornithology, listing three separate references from the journal of *Condor*.

At the reference desk at the library next day, I requested copies of these publications. Within a week, I held in my hand the long awaited answer to my questions.

The first account described a scrub jay picking ticks from a mule deer on March 22, 1944, at Potwisha, at the junction of the Marble Fork and the Middle Fork of the Kaweah River in Sequoia National Park.

Dr. C. M. Herman, Donald McLean of the California Fish and Game, and Clarence Fry, a Ranger of the National Park Service, watched a jay descend and land on the back of a mule deer and hunt for ticks as the deer continued to eat green grass under an oak tree. The deer seemed to welcome the attention rather than resist it. According to local people, this was a daily occurrence, but it was the first time reliable spectators had witnessed and documented the relationship.

My heart began to race when I read there had been four different sightings of scrub jays presumably taking ectoparasites from the back of mule deer near Alpine Lake in Marin County. The reports were in 1970. Our encounter took place in 1978 and only two miles from Alpine Lake.

There were other additional sightings near the Palomarin Field Station of the Point Reyes Bird Observatory, five of them involving single jays and three involving pairs of jays.

In all these incidents, the typical interaction between a jay and a deer involved a jay alighting on the neck, head, or back of a deer and proceeding to clean the animal's head, ears, back, hind limbs, tail, and antlers.

Two different types of pecks were used. One was forceful, the other softer, usually preceded by a short waiting period. These different pecks were thought to be for different food sources.

Throughout the entire process, the deer remained motionless. On three occurrences, the deer extended their ears, even though deer are usually sensitive around the ears. In all cases, the jays would call before and after the grooming, but never during the interaction.

In North America, instances of proto-cooperation are scarce. Cattle egrets, cowbirds, and blackbirds are often seen perching on the back of cattle. But it is thought these birds usually stay in close proximity to cattle because they are able to take advantage of the insects stirred up by the cattle's movement.

Jays are highly intelligent birds with well-developed learning capabilities. Scrub jays remain with their parents for five months and learn a great deal during that time. Thus, it is thought that young jays could pick up this action from their parents and, after they depart their natal territory, teach this behavior to other jays.

Though many sightings of this interaction between a jay and deer have been documented, it does appear to be rare, taking place between late winter to spring when the tick population is more numerous.

The third publication discussed the video tape one photographer in a blind took of a Florida scrub jay foraging on a white-tailed deer. Biologists had rarely had the opportunity to observe this activity, making the video highly valuable.

Until a few thousand years ago, large species of herbivorous mammals representing many families over millions of years lived on planet Earth. Perhaps some scrub jays have a primitive memory of taking advantage of the food source these huge creatures carried with them. Perhaps there is an innate tendency for some scrub jays to be fearless around the deer.

Whatever the reason, I am pleased I have the memory of witnessing this wonderful and rare interaction between the scrub jay and the deer.

The Race to Save a Rail

The year was 1981, and I was a senior flight attendant flying the South Pacific route. Continental Airlines had just added Guam to their list of destinations and having never been to that island, I bid for the route and was able to hold it.

For several months, my friend Vicki and I flew the route – an all-night flight from Honolulu, with a beach-front hotel on a beautiful bay. We would arrive at the hotel early in the morning and immediately hit the water for a swim with our snorkels and fins. After a crowded flight, it felt good to enter that silent ethereal world and let the cool water bathe away our exhaustion, awakening our groggy minds and stretching our cramped bodies. It was there I swam with my first sea snake. After our swim, we would go to the local restaurant and order fried lumpia and San Miguel beer before going to bed for a nap.

One trip, however, we decided to see the island and a few of us flight attendants rented a car. It wasn't the best day for a drive, however. Ominous black clouds in the sky cracked open, allowing silver light to shine down on the gray ocean.

We were traveling through a flat farm area when I saw something skitter across the road. I yelled for my co-worker driving the car to stop.

It had disappeared, but soon there was another movement disappearing into the grassy areas. It was dark for daytime, and the rain was coming down steadily. We sat for just a moment before we saw another movement, and this time I saw a small brown flightless bird moving so fast, it reminded me of a wind-up toy going full speed.

As we drove through that grassy field, we must have seen 15 to 20 of these little brown birds. I didn't identify them until I got home.

The birds we had seen were the Guam rail.

Little did I know that three years later, the Guam rail would be listed as an endangered species and the last one to be seen on Guam would be five years later in 1986. Most experts believe the Guam rail to be extinct in the wild. It formerly ranged over the entire island of Guam, a U.S. territory in the western Pacific.

The major factor in the Guam rail's extinction was the introduction of the brown tree snake after World War II. The brown tree snake is thought to have arrived in Guam hidden in a cargo ship from the New Guinea area. Fast to proliferate, the snake was first sighted in the 1950s, soon became conspicuous throughout central Guam in the 1960s, and by 1968, they were thought to be dispersed throughout the island.

Up to 13,000 snakes per square mile may occur in some forested areas in Guam. With those odds, the small flightless brown birds barely stood a chance.

However, the brown tree snake didn't dine on rails alone. They virtually wiped out 12 species of birds, some found nowhere else, and still other bird species hang on by a thread before they too become extinct.

The population of Guam rails plunged from an estimated 80,000 birds in 1968 to 100 birds in 1983. The U.S. Fish and Wildlife Services, along with a consortium of American Zoo Aquarium Institutes, captured the remaining rails along with the Micronesian kingfisher for a captive propagation program. Guam rails are prolific breeders when left alone, and it's hoped the program can produce 100 rails a year for reintroduction projects while maintaining a population of 150-175 birds in zoo facilities.

On the island of Rota, located only 31 miles north of Guam in the Commonwealth of the Northern Mariana Islands, Guam rails are finding a new home by reintroduction. While the rails are not native to Rota, they are safe since there are no brown tree snakes and the island offers large areas of rail habitat. It is hoped that a wild population on

Rota will ensure that rails can be successfully reintroduced to Guam once the snake population is controlled.

I will never forget seeing so many of these brown stubby-winged flightless birds resembling grouse, teetering off into the high grassy areas. And I will never forget the shock and despair I felt only five years later when I heard they were gone possibly forever.

The brown tree snake now threatens many other islands, including Oahu, with the same devastation.

It's All in a Song

Several years ago, when my husband was teaching art at San Francisco State, he would lead a spring birding walk every year around the campus.

It was on one of these walks that a group witnessed a most unusual incident.

We heard the breeding song of a white-crowned sparrow, high in a tree. As we put our binoculars to our eyes and focused, instead of a white-crowned sparrow, we were looking at a song sparrow.

No doubt about it – this streak-breasted sparrow with a large black spot in the middle of his breast was singing the song of the white-crowned sparrow. How could this be possible, we pondered? Are bird songs inherited or are they learned?

Ornithologists and birders have asked this question for years. The evidence they've gathered is that some songs are completely hereditary while others are learned. In learning songs, birds must have the ability to imitate.

In some birds, that ability can be extraordinary.

But how did a song sparrow raised by a pair of song sparrow parents learn to sing a white-crowned sparrow song? No one will know for sure, but many people can speculate on it and did.

Luis Baptista, Ph.D., chair and curator of ornithology and mammalogy at the California Academy of Sciences, is especially known for his long-term research on how birds learn songs. He was called and came out to record this particular sparrow.

His theory was that this song sparrow was probably raised close to a white-crowned sparrows' nest and may have heard their breeding song more often than he heard his own parents sing their song.

These two calls are distinctively different. The song sparrow song begins with a few short notes and then trills. Some people have often compared the first three notes of his call to the first three notes of *Beethoven's Fifth Symphony*. According to Thoreau, many old country people described the call: *Maids, maids, maids, hang up your tea kettle-ettle-ettle.* The white-crowned sparrow's song begins with a sad plaintive whistle, descending into a trill.

How did this affect the bird that had learned the wrong song?

Unfortunately, he probably never did find a mate. A female white-crowned sparrow may have responded with curiosity to his song. However, she would lose interest immediately when she saw this strange bird of a feather singing the right song.

A female song sparrow would have nothing to do with his appearance, no matter how stunning he may appear, if he continued to sing a strange song that did nothing for her hormonal response.

A Game of Cat and Mouse

A series of severe weather storms had brought several shorebirds inland.

We had heard from birding friends that these poor birds knew nothing about cars and people, and many of them had been killed on the roads. So we drove to Salmon Creek to see what had blown in and set up our telescope.

A Northern Harrier flew down and scooped up a weary phalarope and began to play a deadly game with it. The harrier snatched the pathetic bird from the ground, flew a short distance up and then dropped it. The phalarope tried to escape, only to be plucked up and pecked at again and again.

We watched the phalarope flap with broken wings, only to be tormented over and over by the harrier who continued to play this game of cat and mouse.

A tear slid down my cheek, and I heard myself saying, "Please get it over with."

The game lasted approximately 10 minutes, before the hawk finally tired of it and flew off, leaving the broken bird to die.

The Power of Ospreys

*H*e hovered above the coastline, struggling against the wind. There were no cars behind me, so I slowed down and kept even with him. Powerful wings beating strong as he continued to fight the wind so he could take a huge round grouper home for dinner. Slowly, the osprey began moving in my direction. My sun-roof was open, and I watched as the bird floated directly above me.

Then the thought occurred to me that if he were to drop the struggling fish, I would either have dinner or be dead.

Since my move to the Russian River, the osprey became one of my favorites of the order *Falconiformes*. I loved watching them glide over the water, wings beating, legs trailing, then plunging feet first into the river with tremendous splashes, sometimes almost disappearing. There is always the suspenseful moment waiting to see if the bird would rise out of the water with a slippery victim held tightly in his talons or if he missed.

Although ospreys eat fish almost exclusively, I know from firsthand experience they will eat other birds.

I was driving along the coast one day and watched an osprey fly from inland towards the ocean. The bird was grasping something in his talons, and as he flew closer, I was amazed to see that his prize appeared to be a mourning dove. He was holding the bird head first, belly up, just as he would have held a fish.

Many birding friends seemed skeptical when I mentioned the incident, but according to the *Audubon Encyclopedia of North American*

Birds, ospreys are known to also "catch rodents, snakes, frogs, storm-petrels, sandpipers, ducks, possibly at times when fishes are not available."

I spent one birthday at Lake Manzanita on Mt. Lassen, watching them fish. I thought about all the fishermen who pay for a fishing license, patiently wait in hopes of catching something, and when they did, they had to let it go. All this effort for the fun of it.

I chuckled as an osprey dove down, retrieved a protesting fish with his deadly talons and flew off with it – with no intention of letting it go, without a fishing license, and definitely not for the fun of it.

Little Executioners

The deck was a flurry of movement.

Approximately 50 dark-eyed juncos were busy grubbing for insects and larvae, and looking for seeds that had escaped the bird feeders. Little gray birds, wearing black or dark hoods in the fashion of executioners, continued to scurry about my patio, sending each other visual signals with a flash of white outer tail feathers. Although their hoods appeared foreboding, their soft finch-like pink beaks softened their demeanor.

Whoosh! A dark shadow appeared, and in the instant it took me to blink, the birds were gone – with the exception of one.

A sharp-shinned hawk had made a dive and missed, leaving only a few feathers floating in the air. I slid open the sliding-glass door and peered outside. One terrified junco had seen the clutches of death and escaped. It took off from under the large-leaved plant it had managed to hide behind.

A young sharp-shinned hawk moved into the tree above my bird feeder for a few days, and my feeder sat quiet for a week after he decided to leave. That incident happened several years ago while I was living in a dense residential area in Manhattan Beach in Southern California.

I witnessed another incident years later with my husband in Northern California. Again, the deck was covered with juncos, busy with great activity, flashes of white tails flicking signals of excitement.

Suddenly, they all froze solid. It became dead quiet, and not one of the birds stirred. Some were looking down, while others posed in different positions.

We continued searching the sky and trees, looking and listening for anything to explain this bizarre behavior. Nothing was or ever did become apparent to the cause of the mystery; yet I'm certain there had been a definite threat to the flock.

Suddenly, at what appeared to be the exact moment in time, the birds resumed their movements and search for food. My husband looked at his watch again and said, "They froze for five minutes."

Another favorite dark-eyed junco story is about one particular male. He was easy to spot from the others because instead of wearing the dark executioner hood, he wore a white one like the Ku Klux Klan. My husband and I watched this partially albinistic bird sing, court, and successfully attract a female. We saw him with nesting material and eventually feeding young.

We watched this bird go through the breeding process successfully for two years in a row.

How Birding Saved My Life

In 1986, I was home visiting my parents in Highland, above San Bernardino, California. My mother was dying, and I was there to help my father and spend a last few precious hours with my mother.

My parents lived directly behind the foothills, and behind their house, a marvelous canyon climbs all the way up to Big Bear. My husband and I always looked forward to hiking this canyon when we were visiting. California thrashers are numerous, and we have often seen many desert birds such as Scott's orioles, black-chinned hummingbirds, phainopepla, and lazuli buntings, to name a few.

Feeling depressed, closed-in and trying to come to grips with grief, I got my binoculars and decided to take a walk up into the canyon.

I didn't tell my dad where I was going. He would have worried had he known I was heading for the canyon by myself. He had told me stories about someone finding a dead man and of wild dogs being in the canyon, but I refused to be held hostage to fear of the unknown.

I walked up the ridge and looked down on a lovely old hacienda-style house. I was glad to see someone was restoring it. A large dog started barking, and the owner called him down. I continued to climb up the ridge, then descended to the wash.

It felt good to be outdoors. I looked up at the sky and took some deep breaths. Up ahead, I could see where the wash ended and the canyon began to narrow where vegetation grew.

I had walked approximately half the length of a football field when I suddenly saw a movement in the brush far ahead. Lifting my binoculars to my eyes, I started scanning. My binoculars focused on a large dog.

Then I realized that there was another dog to the left of him, another one to the right and two more behind him. All of them were large and alert – and looking directly at me.

My heart began pounding as the taste of fear rose in my dry mouth.

Slowly, I turned my binoculars around in my hand so I could use them as a weapon. I took a step backwards, then another one. The dogs sprang forward, and the race was on.

I spun around, running faster than I've ever run in my life. I could hear the dogs barking, closer and closer. Something strange happened then. I heard a voice tell me that if I reached the ridge, the dogs would stop the chase because they would be entering the territory of the domestic dog back at the hacienda.

The blood raced through my head, almost drowning out the sound of the dogs. I could see the ridge getting closer and closer.

At last, I scampered up and then slid down the hill towards the hacienda on the seat of my pants. I leaped up and turned around.

The feral dogs had reached the top of the ridge only a few seconds after I slid down, and they stood staring at me. The voice had been right. The chase was over.

His barking German shepherd at his side, the man looked towards me and asked if I was okay. I stood staring at the dogs until finally, the pack leader turned and strutted off; the other dogs followed.

I was numb. My knees wobbled, and I felt sick to my stomach. I stood in the shade holding onto a tree until I had recovered.

I'm absolutely certain the only reason I'm here to write this is because I'm a good spotter. I had seen the flicker of an eye hidden in the brush, and I had seen the movement when it was still far enough away.

Walking back to my parents' house in silence, I thanked the universe I had become a bird watcher, never realizing that one day, my skill in spotting would save my life.

Returning Home

My family eventually moved into a large ranch-style house that sat next to the San Manuel Indian Reservation. Our backyard was visited by an occasional coyote and rattlesnake; roadrunners perched themselves on the fence like sentinels. A deep canyon separated the hills between our home and the reservation.

I remember taking refuge in the canyon when I needed to be alone. A sweet spring bubbled upwards, giving birth to an oasis of lush green plants that contrasted with the golden hills. That was where I watched hooded orioles, California thrashers, lazuli buntings, and goldfinch come down to drink.

And it was also the same canyon where I was chased by five large dogs – and being a good bird spotter saved my life.

When we moved into our new ranch home, I remember wandering through the orange groves and gawking with curiosity at the pathetic hovels where the Indians lived. Rusted pickup trucks roasted in the hot sun, contrasting with pink petunias growing in rusted tin cans in front of their houses.

Native American kids (at that time we called them Indian kids) would come down to raid our neighbors' freezers in their garages, returning home with steaks representing badges of their bravery. They were not welcomed or tolerated in our neat new neighborhood.

My husband and I always looked forward to returning to this canyon when we visited my family together. Our last return to the canyon brought a dumbfounding surprise. On the top of the canyon, where shacks used to be, sat huge new homes with a compound surrounding each home. A huge casino with gaudy lights now stood bright, big and bold where shacks and discarded remnants had once before strewn the land.

What had been a wash we use to cross to reach the canyon trail was now a basin filled with water. We stood watching a shiny black-crested phainopepla taking a bath on the edge of the wash. Dozens of lesser goldfinches sang their sweet mewing songs while feeding on mustard plants. We walked to the end of the road, realizing we were unable to cross the basin to enter the canyon.

Suddenly, a white car with flashing lights slowly made its way to where we stood. Two uniformed Indian security guards got out of the car. One of them announced we were on Indian reservation land.

"I know," I answered. "I grew up here. I used to climb far up into that canyon to hear canyon wren sing and watch lazuli buntings return during migration."

"Not anymore," he answered. "The people who live up there get nervous when they see trespassers down here." He pointed to the new mansions up on the hill.

We shook our heads and laughed in disbelief. My husband asked, "How far over does the Indian Reservation land go?"

The guard informed him they had acquired the land a long way up the canyon. Dennis replied, "Well, why the hell not. Your people were here first."

I will never believe anyone wants to be poor. The casino had brought wealth and status to the San Manuel Indians. Mansions with manicured gardens had replaced the garbage heaps and downtrodden shacks that once stood in front of the canyon. New and expensive trucks had replaced the rusted pickups. I don't begrudge them their new fortune.

But as Dennis and I turned to head back, we paused to watch a ladder-back woodpecker fly across. Suddenly, I felt an immense sense of loss, knowing that I would never be able to enter this canyon again.

Kayaking with Tory

There we sat – my husband Dennis and I – bundled up in wool, fleece and blankets in the camper, listening to it rain hard outside. We were camped at Jenkinson Lake near Pollock Pines in the foothills of the Sierra at 3,500 feet, and our spring trip in search of sun was starting out unseasonably cold and wet.

Our new dog, Tory, a red miniature poodle, accompanied us. It was his first trip in the camper, but he had settled in like a coyote pup settles into a den.

Pleased and happy to include us as part of his pack, he licked us dry with pleasure. We soon found out no place was sacred. Being quite an acrobat, he leaped from the couch to the bed in a single bound.

We got him in February from Poodle Rescue. He was a show dog called "Moonraker making History (Tory)." Unfortunately, he wasn't making history and was sent back east for the Finishes. Forgotten, abandoned and left in his cage, he lost half his weight when someone came to his rescue. We heard of his plight through an internet search and drove 400 miles round-trip to pick him up. Dennis and I were determined to let Tory be a "dog."

The next day the rain stopped, and the birds began to sing at 5 am, causing me to drift in my dreams with notes of the robin's song. I took Tory outside at 6 am and watched steam rise off the jade green lake. A pair of common mergansers disappeared mysteriously into the fog, and a male black-headed grosbeak chuckled and flew across the camp, showing off white bold marks on black wings. Pairs of Canada geese with varying sized babies were enjoying the sun in the green meadow below which was dotted with bright yellow flowers.

We took the kayak out that morning and glided like skaters on polished jade. The reflections of the trees mirrored upside down.

One single male ring-necked duck skirted the edges of the willows, playing hide and seek. We shared the lake with only the geese, a few fishermen, and a pair of cinnamon teal. The male teal stood out like burnished copper.

Our favorite kayak spot was obviously a good fishing spot, too. It was a narrow inlet that became shallower as we headed up towards the waterfall. Willows lined the sides where yellow and Wilson's warblers warbled their similar songs.

We passed the fishermen for the shallower water where we could see several reddish California newts hanging out at the bottom, waiting for a mate to come along. As we leaned over the side in silence, watching the newts, huge trout occasionally came into view.

Tory took to kayaking like children take to baths with rubber ducks. Dennis said, "Get in the boat," and he jumped in behind me. His excitement at seeing some geese caused him to fall overboard. He came up with eyes wide in shock. Dennis had him tethered to a line and pulled him in.

With Tory shivering with cold, we headed back to camp. He must have been properly humiliated because over the next few days, he was more cautious as we paddled.

Our daily walks took us to the waterfall, where a large flume continually emptied white pounding water into the creek. We stood at the base, absorbing the power and feeling the spray's dampness settle on us.

Deep behind us in a hidden glen, I saw rosy pink flowers. Tory and I entered the glen and found the forest floor covered with the fern-like leaves of Dicentra that had given birth to hundreds of bleeding heart bells.

Heading back to the bridge through a shaded area, I spied a sunbeam of light focused on a Solomon's seal plant with its long bold green leaves.

The spray of yellow flowers appeared insignificant compared to the leaves.

These are the treasures of the forest, hidden deep on the floor, saving their loveliness for those who seek to discover.

One day, we drove to Wright's Lake and hiked a mile in the snow to the lake. We watched Tory turn into a river otter as he slithered across white snow patches. The delight we felt watching him was indescribable as he ran, rolled, and disappeared in ice holes to come out the other end.

The happiness of sunny days spent in silent solitude soaring over water like clouds in the sky, discovering a glen of bleeding hearts, and watching a sad misplaced puppy become a dog gave birth to a pleasure in my heart that can only be called joy.

Woodpecker Burn

$\mathcal{W}$e plodded through ash as difficult to walk through as sand on a beach. The smell of smoke hung in the air – even though the fire had been one year ago. Black tree skeletons stood everywhere.

We were in the Sierras, close to the town of Lee Vining on Hwy 120. This burned-out area had attracted a large concentration of woodpeckers, including the elusive and rare black-backed woodpecker.

Dennis had seen the bird only once, several years ago. But I had never seen it, though we had walked many times before in such blackened forests. After a fire, trees often succumb to disease. Insects and larvae move in to feed on the dying trees – and an abundance of woodpeckers soon follow to feast on these creatures.

We read in one of our bird-watching newsletters about woodpeckers being in a burned-out area near Lee Vining. There was a lot of drumming and drilling heard in this spot.

We had been walking now for 30 minutes and hadn't yet heard or seen a woodpecker. I began to fear the birds had left the area.

Then we heard distant pecking.

I had always thought it was relatively easy to spot a woodpecker, but I was surprised how easily the birds blended into the charred and blackened remaining trees.

We chased the pecking and noisy calls, but after seeing ten hairy woodpeckers, my hopes of spotting the black-backed began to wane.

Suddenly we heard a new call.

Focusing our binoculars towards the sound, we were pleased to identify the Lewis' woodpecker, another difficult woodpecker to find.

All glossy black-green on the back with a rosy belly and a dark red face, it sported a pale gray collar. Dennis and I had not seen the Lewis' woodpecker in years. This was a good consolation prize if we didn't see the black-backed.

To add confusion, many mountain bluebirds had moved into the area. White-breasted nuthatches were everywhere, taking advantage of the woodpecker holes for nesting. Babies chased their parents, begging for food.

We kept following woodpeckers, and Dennis proposed we walk over to a denser area of trees. Pointing out a square patch of scrapings on one of the trees, he explained this could definitely be a sign of the black-backed because they prefer to chip off bark to find beetle larvae, instead of excavating holes.

I heard a two-note call I didn't recognize. It sounded like *pick-pick*. The bird flew, and I saw it land on the side of a tree. Through the binoculars, I saw the all-black back, but still it didn't register until I saw the golden crown.

In my excitement, I shouted, "I don't believe it but I'm looking at a black-backed woodpecker!"

Larger than the hairy woodpecker, his head and back were all black, and he had fine black and white stripes on his belly. His throat and cheeks were all white with a black mustache line. But it was the bright golden crown on top of his head that distinguished him as one of the rare woodpeckers in North America.

The black-backed woodpecker is mostly found in the coniferous forests of Canada. Uncommon in California, it can be found in the Sierras. Its habit of chipping bark off the trees to find grubs and beetles may be the reason it is so elusive.

As the dead trees are denuded of their beetle supply, the birds must look for new stands of trees to continue their life cycles.

Dennis gave out an exhilarated hoot and grabbed me in a big hug. We watched the bird for several minutes, until it flew away. I said, "Let's get out of here and go camping."

I looked down at our red miniature poodle and cried out with dismay. Tory was now an ashy ghost-like dog.

We camped at Lee Vining, and I soon discovered that Tory's paws were caked in pitch that had collected an enormous amount of debris containing gravel and hard rocks. After giving him a bath to wash the ash out of his fur, it took me several hours of soaking his feet and pulling between the pads and in-between his toes to be rid of the painful mess.

I felt blessed for finding this special black-backed woodpecker – but sorry Tory had to pay such a painful price for the search.

Finding Solace and Solitude

*L*ast night, I sat in the dark, staring up at the sky and the red sparkling spot called Mars.

As a jetliner flew over the planet, I suddenly realized it was the first jet I had seen in several days since the planes stopped flying. Gazing at the plane, I felt alone, and I was certain the passengers and flight crew must feel lonely too.

Only five days ago, on Sept. 11, 2001, we watched on television the horror of the planes crashing into the Twin Towers of the World Trade Center and the Pentagon, the Towers' collapse, and the plane going down in the Pennsylvania countryside.

The rest of that day was surreal for everyone. Like many others, Dennis and I rushed to give blood. The following day was like having a hangover – unable to focus on anything but the television, forgetting things, even losing a credit card.

The next several days were filled with sadness and tears as we mourned the gigantic loss to this country.

Having been a flight attendant for 18 years, I felt the horror those people must have felt before their death. Many of my flight attendant friends called and said they were plagued with the same hideous thoughts and restless dreams I had been experiencing.

While many Americans hurried to cathedrals, synagogues, and mosques to pray for our country, Dennis and I packed the camper and kayak, and headed with our dog, Tory, for a quiet place to grieve and recover.

As I sat listening to the wind sigh through the treetops, a wave of peace washed over me. I was thankful once again to find comfort and peace in nature. My reflections were continually interrupted with the realization that the victims' loved ones may never know peace again. Our freedom will never be as free again, and our illusion of being safe will never be again.

Everything had changed.

A hairy woodpecker *tapp tapp tapps* on a tree. A tiny brown creeper moves up the side of a tree, its tiny feet on the bark. A red-breasted nuthatch honks its nasal call from high above us.

All these sounds comfort me and give me peace, but I wonder how a family or friend of the victims will ever be able to connect with nature's healing grace again.

A black wasp with a white behind attacks a yellow jacket. The battle is vicious. The wasp is twice the size of the yellow jacket. The yellow jacket screams its buzzy outrage, as the fight continues. Three times they slam against the table, as the yellow jacket attempts to free itself. But the wasp wins the battle and flies high up to the treetops with its victim.

Nature can seem as cruel as the terrorists' acts.

It was mid-week, and we had the campground to ourselves. Early every morning, we took our blue kayak on the water, and the silence – like a calming meditation – was broken only by the rhythm of the paddles slicing through the glassy water. Or Dennis' shout of "Dog overboard!" when Tory got too close to my paddle, and Dennis had to grab the handle on top of Tory's life jacket and plop him back on top of the kayak.

One morning, we took a walk on a trail that followed the lake through high chaparral country.

A kingfisher rattled his call from a perch on a dead snag before taking off. We found a mixed flock of birds, mostly Audubon's warblers, showing off their butter butts. Several red-breasted nuthatches continued to climb the under-parts of trees as they scavenged for insects.

An uncommon warbler, the black-throated gray, and a pair of orange-crowned warblers were following the Audubons. A Bewick's wren peeled out a lively song, causing us to pause and search him out. A large flock of baby bushtits, still covered with soft downy feathers, followed their parents' calls.

We spent a week camped next to the lake, the color of polished jade, to recover and prepare for an uncertain future. As I contemplated going to war, realizing the death, grieving and human suffering that was sure to follow, I grieved for our planet Earth too. God gave us this Garden of Eden, nature's holiest of places to worship. Already scarred and abused, our planet may have to sustain the bombing, fire, and destruction of yet another war.

Little did I ever dream we would be engaged in two wars over ten years time.

Healing Through Nature and Family

*B*etween the traffic of moving cars, a sharp-shinned hawk swooped down Hwy 50. Wings beating wildly to keep its balance and talons extending down, the bird plucked off a female house sparrow in the middle of four lanes of traffic. The hawk took to the air, swirling upwards to safety with its captive dinner.

This bold act of nature was one of my few memories of Lake Tahoe when my husband and I passed through there, returning from somewhere else on our way home several years ago.

Not being into skiing or gambling, I never had much interest in Lake Tahoe. Then about six months ago, my extended family decided to have a family reunion on the South Shore of Lake Tahoe in October. Dennis and I packed for cold nights and warm days, took our binoculars in hopes of seeing a few birds, and loaded the kayak.

This family reunion had been planned many months before another unexpected reunion in August had brought the family together much earlier than intended. My father suddenly woke up on a Sunday morning at 5:00 am and asked my stepmother to call 911. He died a few minutes later from a massive heart attack.

Though he was 81 years old, he was a man who seemed to be in great shape physically, and the entire family thought he would live well into his 90s. He was still working a few days a week in engineering, bowled on Thursday nights, and served as president of his Rotary Club. He was a man who had served his country in World War II, where he won a Bronze Star, and he remained a true patriot especially after 9/11. He was proud of his Irish heritage and was the teller of many tall tales and jokes.

So with great sadness, I headed for the original family reunion planned in October. An only child who lost my mother in 1986, I was left with a giant hole in my heart when my father died. When my father remarried in 1989, my new stepmother treated me as one of her girls, and I became part of a large extended family.

Suddenly, I had gone from being an only child to sharing my father with two other daughters and their husbands, four grandchildren and their new wives and husbands, and an adopted Chinese couple and their two daughters. Unfortunately, because of the earlier unexpected reunion, only half of the family had time off to come to Lake Tahoe.

I rose early my first morning, and with a cup of coffee, took my poodle, Tory, outside. The air was crisp and frosty, and I laughed out loud when Tory began skating down the icy pathway to the boats below the house. The blue water captured the reflection of the sky. Rugged mountains stood in the background while flaming trees announced it was fall.

California gulls sailed past the prominent peaks instead of the ocean. A flicker called and then flew its *dippity-dip* flight across the water, its under-wings matching the fall trees.

The beauty suddenly stunned me with my sense of loss. How my Dad would have loved this place. I could see him gathering his fishing gear to catch the big one of the day.

The sorrow stayed with me through the day until we took the kayak out. Gliding across the pure water and gazing at the spectacular scenery soon sent the grief away. A flotilla of Canada geese caught Tory's attention, and I thought he might fall into the icy cold water.

Back at the house, the younger adults were partying in the hot tub. Jason and Dyan arrived with their black Bouvier des Flandres, the size of a small horse. Brandy and her husband arrived with their three Shelties – bringing the total to six dogs with our Tory and Mom's Tibetan terrier, Panda.

Some members of the family were playing games, and I was in the kitchen, preparing a Spanish vegetable side dish for dinner. Mom came in and gave me a hug. As I chopped onions, the tears began to flow.

Listening to the normal everyday conversation of a family coming together made me realize that besides having given me my life, many material things, and wisdom, my father's best gift to me was this family.

Through nature and this family, the healing had begun.

Rare Bird Alert

The phone call came on the evening of Sunday, February 4th, 2001, from the "rare bird alert" phone tree.

Betty Groce informed me, there was a rare bird out at Stinson Beach. The bird was first located on January 29th by Steve Howell and Sue Abbott during a Point Reyes Bird Observatory (PRBO) census. For three days PRBO called in the experts, who studied the bird.

At first they wanted to call it a Mongolian plover, however, the bill size and shape weren't quite right. No one wanted to be responsible for calling it a greater sand plover, but after a photograph was sent to one of the top definitive plover ornithologists in Britain, he announced after three days that this was indeed a greater sand plover, making it the first of its kind found in North America.

On Monday morning, Dennis and I drove down the coast to catch a glimpse of the bird. A massive white cape of fog shrouded us in its dampness, making it hard to see. Occasionally, pockets of blue sky opened up, warming us with sunlight but only for a few minutes.

Dennis said, "This is great! There's no way we're going to be able to find this bird in fog and with a high tide."

As we approached the gated community Sea Drift Estates, we stopped at the guard gate to receive a pass. Five minutes later, we found a long line of cars parked on the right side of the road. We parked the truck and gazed at the bird watchers. There were 26 birders, 17 telescopes, and five cameras the size of bazooka guns.

"And you had any doubts about finding the bird," I trilled in glee to Dennis.

Richard Hurley, one of our birding companions, smiled and waved to us. We got out and took turns looking through his scope. A medium-size plover, with a heavy bill, white belly and face, and a buff colored back and breast patches, stood on long legs. Someone said it was a second year bird.

How far off had he flown to bring him to this unknown continent, the first of his species to reach North America?

The greater sand plover often is found in large numbers, winters on coasts and estuaries, mostly around the Indian Ocean and Southwest Pacific. It migrates to its nesting grounds and begins nesting in May through August across Eastern Asia from the Himalayas to Northeast Siberia; rarely does it reach Alaska.

That means this bird had flown halfway around the world.

Dennis and I had first seen a greater sand plover at Mai Po in the New Territories of Hong Kong. Though it was not a life bird for us, we could now add it to our ABA, USA, North America, and California lists.

I watched a young man from PRBO wade across the water to the mud flat where the bird had been perched. He picked up two feathers and waded back. I asked him what he planned to do with them, and he said he hoped to run a DNA test on them.

The phenomenon of a bird making the wrong turn and traveling all this way is wild enough to contemplate. But when this happens, there's always another phenomenon that occurs. Betty Groce said there were 50 birders out there to view the bird on Sunday. Some came all the way from New Jersey. I'm sure hundreds of bird watchers saw the sand plover in over the next few weeks.

For most of the birders, the greater sand plover was a life bird. But for me, the pleasure of adding another bird to my life list came when we decided to take a walk down the road.

A palm warbler had been seen in a grove of trees. Several birders were standing in the street, birding the gardens of the Stinson Beach residents.

Suddenly, I heard a man call out, "Cape May warbler."

I took off running towards the bottle-brush trees where the man was pointing. There, hanging upside down, was a streaky bird with a yellow head and yellow on its side.

Bingo, I thought, my life bird for today.

The Cape May warbler is rare west of Texas during migration. It breeds in northern states and in Canada. Since Dennis and I have seen many palm warblers and have them on both our life and California lists, we decided to go have lunch. Our friend Richard stayed, and later we heard he had found the Palm warbler, making it three life birds in one day.

This was a great day in any birder's book.

Kayaking the Estero Americano

*D*ennis put the truck in gear, and we went sliding through the rough road spraying mud everywhere.

We were the third vehicle to get through, with seven more to follow, after leaving the paved road of Estero Lane. We entered the open gate that would take us over a steep dirt road to where we put-in our kayaks and canoes to explore the Estero Americano.

For years, Dennis and I had wanted to kayak this remote stretch of Marin and Sonoma coastlines. We had finally obtained access through Land Paths, an organization that negotiates with private lands for public access. The Sonoma County Agricultural Preservation and Open Space District, as well as the California State Coastal Conservancy, provided funds for the Sonoma Land Trust to purchase the Estero Preserve, which comprises 120 acres of property along the Estero near the mouth of the Pacific Ocean.

Because of its natural beauty and appeal to migratory waterfowl, shorebirds, raptors, songbirds, and 45 species of fish including steelhead and salmon, the Estero is considered one of the most important biological areas in Northern California.

My first look down at the estuary made me think about New Zealand with its unique fjord-like views.

Our friend, Peter Leveque, was to be our naturalist. He is a retired Sonoma State Biologist and always brings a good sense of humor to those lucky to bird or kayak with him. He started the day off by telling us about traveling with a geologist friend who wasn't interested in birds. Peter called out for his friend to stop as he had seen a bird perched. He got out of the car and discovered it was a turkey vulture. Not wanting to admit to his friend he had stopped for a vulture, Peter told his friend it was a red-headed eagle, and his friend was impressed. For the rest of the day, people were calling out red-headed eagles when they spotted turkey vultures.

Finally, we were gliding over the smooth water, dipping our paddles and heading up the Estero. The day was overcast, but not too cold for a February afternoon, and we were all pleased the trip hadn't been rained out.

Huge flocks of bufflehead kept moving as we approached them, showing off their bold black and white plumage. Looking up at a vibrant green pasture, I was pleased to see several meadowlarks, a bird I use to take for granted because their numbers were so numerous. Today, they are in trouble as their habitat is disappearing.

A wrentits' call bounced across the estuary like a ball. A pair of bufflehead flew above our kayak so close I could hear their wings whistling. We stopped at a wall and looked up at two small cave-like holes where a barn owl had been seen several times with babies. It appeared abandoned this time.

We decided to turn back and head to the beach.

A pair of red-tailed hawks played their mating games that appeared more like deadly war games as the male descended fast on the female, their talons touching in a lethal circle dance.

Suddenly, a large dark falcon came into view, and Dennis called out, "Peregrine falcon!" Instead of streaking by with incredible speed as usual, this one seemed to almost hover before dipping down and out of view.

The sound of surf and roaring waves became increasingly loud as we approached the beach. We gathered with the other birders on the beach, eating our early dinner.

Fresh salty air and hard exercise breeds a healthy appetite. Some folks strolled down the beach, bringing back bird skulls and crab skeletons. Some decided to wait for sunset before paddling back to the cars.

Dennis and I decided to leave early since we didn't care to negotiate the muddy trail back up to the gate in the dark. We discovered the tide was going out, and the current was moving so swiftly, we were afraid we would be swept out to sea. Dennis went back to tell the others, and we towed our kayak quite a distance before it was safe to paddle against the current, making for good workout.

We passed a flock of godwits drilling deep with their probing bills in the sand near the shoreline, too occupied with finding dinner to be bothered with us.

As we paddled in to where the vehicles were parked, I looked back and the Estero Americano was tinged in pink. I reflected with gratitude the opportunity to have discovered this beautiful spot of uncommon beauty in our magnificent Sonoma County.

Travel Adventures

California gulls sailing

Past snow-covered peaks

In lieu of the sea

Birds Know No Boundaries

As I handed the immigration officer my passport upon arriving home from Honduras, a thought occurred to me. Birds know no borders and recognize no political peripheries. As we jet-set across coasts and continents, we still must deal with passports, airline tickets, health certificates and excess baggage.

However, a bird can fly from one country to another, winter in the warm tropics and return to the United States to his breeding grounds. Birds seem to understand something we have never understood about freedom of movement.

Entering Syria is a serious business. A visitor might expect to be detained and interrogated if the transit documents have not been properly prepared. Machine guns block entry to many countries. The borders in Eastern Europe have changed faster than I can keep up, and the waste of war and rebellion upheaval goes on in the Middle East.

But a bird has only to fly over the border and take up residence. Birds do not recognize political differences.

The same birds that visit or live in Israel have been flying through Palestine long before the Jews and Palestinians began quarreling over land territory. The unmistakable African hoopoe breeds in Europe but winters in Africa while stopping for a rest in Israel. Cattle egrets have expanded their territory by the process of invasion, like Saddam Hussein, but without half the fuss or pollution. Northern warblers ignored the conflicts of the Contras and the Sandinistas and the turmoil of El Salvador.

This contrast of freedom of movement makes our political ploys appear ludicrous.

The Atlantic Ocean in winter seems a lonely and frigid place to be, but the pelagic birds make their home on the rolling sea, just as a meadowlark makes its home in winter on the rolling meadows of America.

The Pacific Ocean is home to albatrosses that sail on the winds as the bald eagles soar in the skies of Alaska. The marshes in Russia are a mass of teeming ducks and shorebirds just like our marshes here at home.

Nature does not know a boundary, a prejudice, or a foreign language; only we do.

Indeed, the mystery of migration of many bird species magnifies the freedom of movement from one continent to another. This intriguing drama has been happening since before the glaciers advanced and retreated.

Bird life existed on this planet for millions of years. This thought staggers the mind when we stop and consider time and realize that while we continue to set self-imposed limitations upon ourselves through our prejudice, religious self-righteousness, and political pettiness, something else is taking place.

As we hear the honking of the Canada geese heading north and our heads turn to look towards the sky, we must know that a much larger cosmic magnitude is happening and has been happening for a very long time, and it's much bigger than us.

Farewell to Africa

Stalking a strange bird call, I rounded a bush and almost jumped out of my skin. A tall fierce-looking black man stood in front of me. He wore remnants of a rag-a-tag uniform and carried a large rifle. "Jambo," he said.

"Jambo," I answered, a little shaky.

"You must go back to the lodge. It is not safe for you to be out here by yourself," he reminded me.

It was my last day on safari, and we had just arrived at a lovely English colonial hotel, the Nugulia Lodge in Tsavo, Kenya, East Africa.

The scrub habitat always seemed to lure me further away from the safe garden areas and civilization of the lodges. Even though I had seen and heard the crunching of bones and roar of lions at night, I never gave it a thought that they could be my bones the lions could be chomping on.

I decided to take a different path back to the lodge and was glad I did. A large tree was bursting with activity and noisy chatter. Weaver birds were busily building their intricate basket nests, weaving dry grass strands into masterpieces as fine as any complex basket. Glancing through my book, I identified my last bird on my ten days of safari – black-headed weaver birds.

That night after dinner, sad to be saying farewell, I wandered out onto the terrace to see if any animals had come to the salt lick that evening.

Only one lone elephant stood at the lick. Watching her, I wondered how long her ancestors had walked these dry plains where man was born. Would there be room on the planet for her species in the next century?

Suddenly, she looked up, ears waving like antennas, glancing in my direction. The terrace was two stories high, and she continued to stroll towards the compound until she stood directly in front of me, about six feet away. We looked at each other eye-to-eye.

I heard other people moving backward anxiously, softly gasping. Someone tugged at my arm, trying to gently move me away. I stood my ground and continued gazing into her small, wise eyes, feeling a primal sense of awe, respect, and love for this enormous creature.

There was no doubt we were communicating.

After a few minutes, she raised her trunk up in the air and saluted me. I raised my arm in salute to her and Africa. Slowly and gracefully, she backed up and turned around, disappearing into the darkness.

That was in October, 1974, just seven years after the Mau Mau uprising, where the black man began taking back his land from the European colonizers. I was the only bird watcher on our safari and relatively new at the game. I returned with an embarrassing low number of bird species – and memories that would last a life time.

Africa with her blazing sunsets that rivaled the bright colors worn by the tall proud Maasai people. The smell of pungent raindrops cooling the dry cracked earth, and the sound of savage screams at night. I will never forget the African drum beat. It was a spiritual trip into the unknown that connected me to a new primal side of myself.

The last entry in my journal reads, "We drove back to Nairobi and stopped at Zimmerman's Taxidermist and Skins Factory."

It was there that I realized the fragility of everything we had seen.

Piles of zebra skin rugs lay sprawled on the floor, on sale for $75 each. Stiff carcasses in ghastly poses barely resembled the live and vital animals we had observed the past 10 days. An elephant foot supported an ashtray. I felt revulsion as I watched people I had come to know over shared dinners laughing and buying zebra rugs and trophies.

We left there, and I immediately walked to the East African Wildlife Society and bought myself a life membership.

Lost Cities and Amazon Jungles

In September 1976, I flew to Lima, Peru for a two-week vacation. I was a flight attendant at the time and had booked an airline excursion tour that was just for airline personnel. My itinerary included visiting the white volcanic city of Arequipa, a train ride over the Andes to Lake Titicaca – the highest lake in the world – Cuzco and Machu Picchu, and two nights' stay at Amazon Lodge on the famous Amazon River.

I couldn't afford the expensive bird watching tours that I doubt were even in existence then.

I was a beginning birder and was totally unprepared for birding on my own in a new destination. At that time, there was only one book written for birding South America, The Birds of South America by Rodolphe Meyer de Schauensee. It was a hard-bound and awkward to carry for field study. The few illustrations of birds that it did offer were poorly drawn. I had to depend on notes taken during the day and reading text to identify the birds I saw. It was a long, tedious process that most often ended with no confirmation on the birds I had seen.

Needless to say, my list was small since I listed only the few birds I was completely sure I had seen. My grand total came to 20 birds. It's painfully embarrassing to admit that, but I was new at birding, alone, and the territory was largely unexplored.

After reading Richard Haliburton's romantic description of "the Lost City of the Incas" in his book The Royal Road to Romance, I knew I had to see Machu Picchu. It was every bit as mysterious and magnificent as I had imagined, and it was the only time I felt I truly stood on top of the world.

My bird list doesn't mention any birds seen there. I prefer to think that I was completely captivated with the energy of Machu Picchu, and for once, forgot the birds.

We boarded a boat that took us up the Amazon River to the Amazon Lodge. It was my first time in a rain forest, and I fell passionately in love with the wildness of it.

I have been traipsing through jungles ever since. I will never forget waking up to the strange calls of birds, beckoning me to come outside. I saw many colorful and strange birds but my list has the only two birds I was able to identify easily – the lesser kiskadee and the mountain cacique.

Our guide led us along a narrow trail through the jungle to visit a small village of the Yagua Indians. Just 20 years earlier, they had been dangerous head-hunters, and I remember being appalled at seeing small black shrunken heads hanging from their windows. We watched men demonstrate blowing poison darts through long blow-guns. I was unprepared to trade with the Indians and rummaged through my purse to find something. I found an old mirror and held it up to bargain.

Immediately, a small brown woman with a wrinkled face came forward, pushing her husband to do the negotiating. As she peered into the mirror, her dry cracked face broke into a wide smile with few teeth, and she was transformed into a young shy girl. She said something to her husband unintelligible to me, and he presented a necklace made of seed pods. I accepted the necklace and put it around my neck. We both nodded in agreement, and they stepped away; the bargain was sealed and completed.

The Yagua people were already in trouble then from their culture colliding with civilization. We saw many small children with distended tummies from malnutrition and skinny dogs. I didn't understand at the time how this was possible in a Garden of Eden filled with flowers, roots, and animals to eat.

My naïveté matched the ignorance of the entrepreneurs that invaded this land and the vulnerability of the Yagua people.

I later understood that endangered species included endangered peoples.

The King of Birds

There is a Mayan folk tale that tells the story of how the resplendent quetzal outsmarted the roadrunner and became the "king of birds."

However, any international birder knows why this bird is really king. It is probably one of the most beautiful birds in the world.

The resplendent quetzal is found in Central America in a few of the cloud rain forests that are still left standing. It is a member of the Trogon family, and with the male's streaming tail feathers, it can be as much as 25 inches long. The male bird is a glittering green with an intense contrast of color; he boasts a brilliant red belly with white under-tail coverts.

For years I hoped that one day, I would go to the high forests in search of this bird. I even had a friend of mine paint the resplendent quetzal on my telescope.

In 1988 my husband Dennis and I took off for Costa Rica to make this dream come true.

We rented a Russian jeep that we soon discovered drove more like a tank, and we named it "Gorby" as we drove up to Monteverde Cloud Forest. The last three hours of the drive was up a dusty dirt road, and with all the stops we made for bird watching, we arrived in the small town of Monteverde in the late afternoon.

We rented a small cabin and made ourselves comfortable. When the evening air turned cool, we moved inside from the porch to finish our bird checklist for the day.

It was dark when we decided to go to dinner, and I stepped off the porch expecting to find the stairs. The ground came up fast, and I hit it hard with a loud *thunk*. The air was sucked out of me, and agonizing pain poured through me.

Eventually I was able to sit up. I had sprained a wrist but more importantly, I had smashed my right kneecap, and I was in a great deal of pain. The restaurant did not have any ice, so my husband used cold water to stop the swelling. I took some codeine and went to bed.

The next morning, I insisted on taking Las Cascadas trail up to where we hoped the quetzals would be. It was rough climbing this narrow trail through the rainforest, and it was only perseverance and strong intestinal fortitude that helped me make it.

We came upon a small group of other bird watchers and birded with them for a short time.

Suddenly, Dennis said excitedly, "Oh, I've got something!" He began to describe the bird, but it wasn't until he got to the green streaming tail that he realized he was looking at a resplendent quetzal.

His expression of awe and surprise made my pain go away for one brief moment.

The bird flew to another branch, and I watched the gleaming green iridescent feathers floating behind a brilliant bird. The forest was filled with the soft intakes of breath and exclamations from the group of bird watchers. Soft melodious calls of *k'loo keeloo* delicately punctuated the quiet of the damp forest as two other birds came into view.

We walked a round trip of six or seven miles that day, and during the last mile back to the cabin, I was crying out loud from the pain. My knee was as swollen as an elephant's foot, and I thanked the Universe I had brought codeine with me on the trip.

I often wondered if I would have climbed that mountain for any other bird. Looking back on it, I would probably say no. But for the "king of birds," I would do it again.

Fading into the Pink Sunset

While in Peru in 1976, there were few roads, and much of our travel was by planes and trains. I remember staring out the train window at a stark land with no trees, at an elevation of 12,500 feet.

Lake Titicaca, the highest large navigable lake in the world, appeared to have been dropped from space.

We visited the Uros Indians, who lived on Lake Titicaca on floating islands made of reeds. Everything they owned was made of reeds – including their houses, beds, and boats. Every time we moved, the ground wobbled, as if we were walking on a giant water-bed.

I saw Puna ibis and Andean geese at Lake Titicaca.

Sharp biting cold air made it difficult to breathe at that elevation, and it seemed peculiar to be so cold at such lofty elevations and not see snow.

It was easy to understand the Peruvian natives' passion for color in this frigid land, though. The women wore five and six layers of skirts and sweaters, all in different bright colors and designs. Long black braids dangled down their backs, and black derby hats perched on their heads. Many carried babies swaddled in bright material suspended on their backs, and they were forever spinning wool with a simple hand device.

We departed Puno by train, following Lake Titicaca for many miles.

It was there that I saw a large flock of Andean flamingos.

A snow-capped mountain stood in the distance, the only contrast to the barren lake and wasteland. Suddenly, small shadows of many tall birds tinged in pink began to materialize. As we came closer, their huge bills and black butts became visible. But the color pink in that icy blue and gray landscape told me that no place is forgotten in nature.

Compared to the many other species of flamingos, not much is known about the Andean flamingo. The isolated and rugged habitat and high elevation made it difficult for scientific observation. Little is known about migration patterns. However, a census organized by the Wildlife Conservation Society, in January 1997, discovered the Andean flamingo population is dropping to a disturbing low.

The volcanic mountains and salty lagoons where the birds live have been polluted by increased mining of borax, lithium, and other chemicals.

Environmental hazards from mining change the water levels in the lagoons.

Adventure travel tourism has increased and caused stress on the flamingos. Removal of eggs for food is illegal but still occurring and with the other risk factors is now detrimental to the birds. Roads are now being built in the remote Andes, unlike when I was there, and this has allowed predators such as foxes to invade new territories.

In the mid-1970s, a census placed the Andean flamingos at 150,000.

Assessments are difficult today and may vary greatly but it is estimated that their numbers are somewhere between 50,000 and 100,000 and declining every year. Also, there are fewer nesting colonies.

The Andean flamingo has a longevity average of 50 years. If their environment continues to be assaulted, these birds may be the last generation of their species. It will take a cooperative conservation effort of Bolivia, Chile, Peru, and Argentina to save this magnificent bird.

Nature did not forge to paint the flamingos pink, so they could be the exclamation marks in this remote land. Only man has forgotten and now the pink Andean flamingos may be fading fast into their final pink sunset.

A Pelican Frenzy

We had driven a Volkswagen over the high mountains from Oaxaca to the coast. It took us six long hours, and we were hot and out of steam when we arrived at the lazy Mexican beach resort of Puerto Escondido.

The minute we got into our room, I jumped into my swimsuit and headed for the beach. The cool water was gloriously refreshing. An older gentleman was swimming too, and we began to tread water and converse in an easy relaxed way.

Suddenly, I felt my foot hit a fish, and then the ocean exploded around us. I froze with fear.

I looked up and saw a hundred pelicans swarming down on us. Some were landing as close as two feet away. Splashes were erupting everywhere, and in the center of this hysteria, I realized that they were swooping in on a school of fish, and we were in the middle of a feeding frenzy.

Pelicans are among the largest of living birds, and to see these primitive-looking birds with a wingspan of six to seven feet descend next to me made me think of old black-and-white horror movies where prehistoric flying reptiles swooped down and snatched the poor human victim, usually a screaming woman, to fly away and never be seen again.

Then understanding replaced panic, and I watched in awe as pelicans scooped up fish with what appeared to be gallons of water. They would hold the fish momentarily in their pouch, long enough to squeeze the water out of the corners of their mouths, then tilted their head upwards, and I'd see the fish through the thin skin of their pouch disappear down their throats.

I dove down to see what this chaos must look like from beneath the surface, and the exploding noise was muffled immediately. I looked up to see bobbing bodies with long legs and webbed feet with long toenails.

The water erupted with turbulence as a pelican dove down next to me, snatching up one of many silver flashes, then propelling himself upwards to the surface with strong webbed feet.

I have no idea how long this frenzy lasted but when it finally ended, it stopped as suddenly as it began. I looked at the older gentleman, who peered back at me in shock, and I yelled a huge emotional war-whoop and waved my arms in excitement.

I felt alive and vital but mostly I felt privileged to have shared such a moment with these magnificent birds.

Birding China on the Sly

$\mathcal{B}$ack in April 1995, we took a trip to Thailand and Hong Kong, and we planned to bird Mai Po Swamp managed by World Wildlife Fund. Armed with our permits and insect repellent, my husband, our dear friend Ann Shadwick, and I set off at 7 am.

Mai Po is located at the northern most point in the New Territories, right next to China. We took a cab to the Kowloon train station and boarded a train to Sheng Shui. From there, we caught a bus west to the Mai Po Reserves. The walk to the entrance of Mai Po from the bus stop was approximately one mile.

We spent too much of our first day at Mai Po studying the LBJs (little brown jobs), and when the high tides came, we had missed most of the shorebirds. We promised to pay attention the next day. We also discovered that the best shore birding was on the other side of the twenty-foot high fence on the border, and we needed a Frontier Pass to enter. We had the Mai Po permits but didn't have the Frontier Pass and no time to obtain one.

The next day was a repeat trip getting to Mai Po. We all knew what we wanted to do, but none of us had mentioned it. We birded our way over to the wire fence. The sign said violators would be prosecuted but there were no guards in the "Check Point Charlie" towers.

We all looked at each other and smiled – and then opened the big heavy gate by sliding the bolt and entered China without a permit.

There was a long boardwalk, and we began walking what seemed to be a distance as far as Shanghai. At the end of the boardwalk was the longest blind I have ever seen. Adjusting our breathing to the tight

121

closed air and our eyes to the darkness, we realized there were some 25 other hardcore birders in there, and they made room for us at one end of the blind.

I felt the excitement of the unknown as I sat staring through my binoculars at Deep Bay with Chinese ships passing an unknown city with high-rise buildings and a smaller replica of the Eiffel Tower.

The blind was filled with representatives from many nations, mostly men, including Australia, Denmark, Great Britain, Germany and Japan. We were the only Americans.

The Australians knew the birds well, and with their quick wit, kept us informed and quietly chuckling at their dry sense of humor.

There was one gentleman who had been there for 10 days hoping to see what he dubbed "the mythical spoon-billed sandpiper." When we first arrived at the blind, the tide had yet to recede.

An osprey was sitting on a T-bar, and avocets sleepily floated near the blind. A grand white-breasted sea eagle came flying into view. The osprey was outraged when the big guy took over his perch. Three times he dived at the eagle, still holding onto his fish. Eventually, he settled on another perch.

Slowly the tide began to go out, leaving mudskippers flapping in the mud. The osprey and eagle disappeared. In the beginning, it was easy to follow and learn the birds as they were close enough for identification. There were redshanks, curlew sandpipers, watercocks, Australian curlew, common and spotted greenshanks, to name a few. Even the names were new.

But as the tide went further and further out, more and more birds were coming in but landing too far to be identified. It was extremely hot and difficult to breathe.

I finally gave up trying to identify faraway spots on the water and told Ann and Dennis I would meet them back at the center for lunch. The fresh air felt good, and I enjoyed watching crabs dig holes as I walked back along the boardwalk.

But when I got to the gate, I couldn't get the bolt to slide from the other side. For one panicky moment, I thought they've locked us all in China and we would never see home again.

Then I tried again and it gave way.

I'm sure no one in the blind had a permit. Only bird watchers would be so foolhardy, I thought, as we headed back to Hong Kong on the train, having birded Red China on the sly.

Out of Disaster, A Refuge

We donned rubber boots for a walk through the mangrove. Oozy black mud sucked at our feet, making slurping noises and spewing mud droplets everywhere as we walked. Looking like vines, mangrove roots attached themselves to the mud like octopus legs.

We were near the town of Tarcoles in Costa Rica, and staying next to the Tarcol River where it runs into the Pacific Ocean.

An alluring yellow bird with a bright chestnut head flitted in front of us. The mangrove warbler makes his home with the mangrove vireo. We also found Tennessee warbler, Philadelphia vireo, gray-crowned yellowthroat, and the wren that is called the plain wren and is anything but plain.

We left the humid and oppressive mangroves for the open sky and headed for the beach. The hot sun was tempered with a cool sea breeze. At first sight, the beach looked like a prime piece of real estate from the developers' point of view.

And then the garbage began to appear.

Discarded plastic bottles were mixed with cloth materials, torn canvas, disintegrating boots, a woman's high-heel shoe, a child's small sandal, torn blankets, discarded toys. The mounds of trash covered a mile of what was pristine beach.

Our guide, Kevin Easley, told us these were all the belongings washed up from the victims in the aftermath of the powerful Hurricane Mitch in October, 1998.

A child's plastic doll holding a plastic baby bottle still in one piece tugged at my heart. I was staring at the graveyard of what were once the loved and needed possessions of a people who had lost everything – possessions that had survived the war of storm to be deposited on foreign shores.

Kevin knew I needed a collared and Wilson's plover, and I knew his determination to find me one by now. We weren't leaving without it.

We walked towards the opening of the river and sure enough, there was one Wilson's plover.

We continued walking through the remains of personal property. The sweltering heat was scorching. We had lost the sea breeze, and I felt the depression of walking through this waste weighing heavily on me.

Kevin yelled for me to stay clear of some large driftwood branches. "Killer bees," he warned. I looked through my binoculars at the driftwood covered in moving large black bees. I shuddered and moved off.

I wondered why he insisted on continuing in this direction when suddenly he stopped and pointed. "Look at the log between the green and red plastic bottles," he said.

At first, I didn't see anything, and then several black-bellied plovers materialized. A few ruddy turnstones were turning over clods of junk. Two sweet snowy plovers were lying in the middle of the debris.

All these birds were enjoying the peace of the camouflage created by the disaster.

Minutes later, Dennis and Kevin spotted my bird, the collared plover. One white plover with a single black even band circled its breast and neck. A chestnut cap graced its head. Big plover-like eyes blinked as it stood moving its head in innocent curiosity. It stood on one fragile pink leg, with one delicate foot raised.

Here amid the ruins of countless lives, it had found a home with many other birds. One country's tragedy had become the birds' refuge.

The Shoebill at Mabamba Swamp

*O*ur guide, Malcolm Wilson, called out, "African orange-bellied parrots up in the vlighia tree."

Not knowing a vlighia tree from a fig tree, I looked to see where he pointed. Then I saw the birds and heard the squawking.

Several parrots sat at the top of a tree, eating what appeared to be red fruit. They were striking birds with orange breasts, greenish backs and brownish heads.

Malcolm reminded me about the fruit we had found in the forest the day before. They were red pods that when opened, exposed three black olive-size seeds. "That's what these parrots eat," he explained.

Shortly after going down the road again, Malcolm told our driver, Alfred, to pull over.

An Abyssinian blue colobus monkey sat in the top of a dead tree, surveying his kingdom. He appeared to be alone. Heavy-built and jet-black over all, he sported a white beard and a conspicuous white mantle of long fur extending from his shoulders to the root of his tail. His long tail looked like a rope tipped in orange.

We were on our way to Mabamba Swamp in Uganda, where we hoped to find one of the most sought after birds in Africa – the shoebill. My first birding mentor was the late Arnold Small, an inveterate world birder. Back in 1976, he wrote about finding his 4,000th world bird, the shoebill. He loved the bird enough to bear its name on his California license plate. I had no idea at the time what a shoebill even looked like. So it was with great anticipation that I hoped to see the shoebill soon.

At Mabamba Swamp, several long canoes were staggered in a narrow lagoon. We hiked out to the end of a dock made of wooden planks and boarded one of the boats. Our oarsman began rowing backwards until he could turn around.

Malachite kingfishers sparkled azure blue. Several of these small kingfishers were sitting quietly on low-hanging bushes in the canal. They were a kaleidoscope of color with azure blue backs, bright orange breasts and large red bills.

Yellow-billed ducks dabbled near the shallows. A large and impressive saddle-billed stork could be seen in the distance. This black and white stork has a long tri-colored red and black bill with pendulous yellow and red wattles.

Another guide in a canoe pulled along side ours and told us the shoebill was there. The excitement increased with the news. This is an extraordinary bird that may be related to the pelicans. Nowhere common and usually scarce, they are the water bird version of the Holy Grail. The other guide asked his French passenger if he minded taking us out to show us the bird. The Frenchman was accommodating.

Our boatman paddled a short distance when Malcolm quietly pointed out the huge head standing above the reeds. The boat turned in that direction and slowly glided up to a place where we could see the complete bird.

A Goliath of a bird, he stood four feet tall, massively bulky and prehistoric in appearance. His huge bill, for which he got the name "shoebill", had a small hook at the tip for helping to catch his prey, the lungfish. He was mostly gray and had a small pointed crest on his head. His orange eyes looked the size of large marbles. He appeared noble and confident and superior to everything else in the swamp. We watched him take several steps forward before taking off with little effort for such a big bird.

We continued to search for other birds.

Jacanas walked on lily pads, while long-toed plovers showed off their bold black and white wing patterns. White-wing terns spiraled and plunged ahead of us.

Malcolm suddenly became excited. Pointing, he called out, "Pygmy geese."

Several small goose-like birds floated quietly. Bright orange on the belly with a dark back and a white face, these birds are misleadingly named, as they are actually a small duck. Rather widespread, they are elusive, usually hiding behind dense vegetation.

Then the wind came up and we headed back to shore. As I enjoyed the memory of seeing this giant goliath bird, the Shoebill, Malcolm pointed out swamp flycatchers, sitting close to stunning malachite kingfishers and blue-breasted bee-eaters; a perfect ending for such a great day.

Gorilla Trekking

I was standing precariously on a rock, ready to try to swing myself up to the next ledge, when Joseph, one of the guides, grabbed my arm and propelled me forward.

The vertical climb up Mt. Kato in the Virunga chain of volcanoes in Rwanda was steep and precipitous, and Joseph had been a guardian angel.

We had made it to the top, and now we entered the dark understory of bamboo and meadows of high grass in pursuit of the gorillas.

We had originally booked a side trip to see the gorillas in Uganda, but all the gorilla permits had been booked up. So we decided to take an extra two days and go over the border to Rwanda. We found out later this was a good thing, because the gorillas in Rwanda were much more habituated to humans.

We had presented our permits and were sent to a guide at one of the five posts. Five groups of no more than seven people were to go up to five different gorilla families. Trackers with GPS helped the guides locate the gorilla groups and guard the gorillas from poachers.

We were thrilled to hear that our group consisted of ten gorillas. We were going to see the largest silverback of all the groups and the youngest baby, only one month old.

As we plodded our way through the dense forest, we saw fresh elephant and buffalo scat and the huge footprints of an elephant. We had two guides with us, followed up by two armed men dressed in camouflage in case of a dangerous encounter. The lead guide kept in contact with the trackers.

When we reached the trackers, we were told to leave our packs and water bottles, and take only our camera and video equipment. Then we began to understand the world as a gorilla sees it, creeping low under the over story.

Suddenly, we came out to an opening and to my amazement, there sat one of the two silverbacks, just a few feet away. He was eating leaves off a long vine, and wasn't the least bit intimidated by us.

Beside another adult were two juvenile gorillas. One of the juveniles began to show some stress when we appeared and walked over to the other juvenile and shoved him.

I couldn't help chuckling – on the way up the bumpy road, Dennis and I had seen a similar interaction between two young children. A small toddler fell down and hit his head; raising himself up and bawling, he walked over to his brother and gave him a push. The similarity between the stressful aggressive behavior of the two human children and just hours later, the two gorilla juveniles, was very amusing to us adults.

The silverback rose and lumbered further into the forest. The entire group followed. We were told to circle around. The spongy dense foliage made it difficult to maintain balance and we kept getting caught up in vines.

As I rose to the top and looked down, there was the mother holding her tiny baby to her breast. She was very protective of the infant, looking up at us every so often.

Dennis had circled around a different way and was below me. But he didn't see the second silverback strolling up behind him and our leader, who were blocking his way. The silverback came to a stop behind Dennis as if he were in line at the movies.

Then he became impatient and started shaking his head from side to side as he shuffled his feet back and forth. Our guide finally looked back at Dennis with surprise, whispered for Dennis to move back. The huge gorilla plodded past them.

Our guide told us to keep climbing to the top and circling around. I was one of the first to make it and moved in tight to make room for the others. The sighting couldn't have been better.

There was the goliath silverback sitting next to a youngster on the edge of the world with a stunning backdrop of mountains, and then the sun came out. It was the same juvenile who had earlier shoved his sibling, and he immediately showed stress as I settled down on my knees about five feet away. He glared at me and moved further away down the hill. I looked down the hill and could see the heads of several gorillas.

The silverback showed how powerful he was by pulling up wild celery by the root and began feeding, as the young ones came in to share the roots.

We were allowed one hour of watching these remarkable creatures and only 720 are left in the wild. These spectacular mountains are home to only 320 mountain gorillas. In Bwindi Impenetrable National Park in Uganda, our next stop, there are only 300.

As I stood watching the male silverback, I couldn't help seeing some intelligence of my primitive past in his eyes. And when his eyes finally rested on mine, I wondered if he saw something similar in me.

REFLECTIONS

I LAY MY HEAD DOWN

ON PILLOWS OF CLOUDS

AND COVER MYSELF WITH A

QUILT OF BLUE SKY

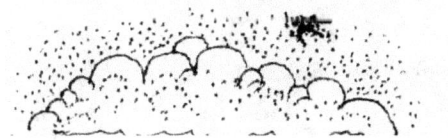

Movement: A Magnificent Mystery

*H*ow can a fragile feathered bird weighing less than 15 grams fly the distance of two or three thousand miles twice a year? What tells a bird in the rainforest that it is time to head north to our redwood forests? The movement of migration is truly a magnificent mystery.

The bird's performance is even more remarkable when we view the accuracy of seasonal timing of its return to their breeding grounds. Even though the stories of the swallows of Capistrano have been greatly distorted, many birds do return every year in the same week – and a few will return the same day.

What makes this extraordinary to me is that migratory birds return more closely correlated with the calendar date than they do with weather conditions that differ every year.

Among the many environmental factors, the key one that probably signals the bird's brain to begin fattening up for the long journey is the length of daylight. Carbohydrates (sugars and starches), proteins, and fats are consumed by birds. Fats store nearly twice as much energy per unit weight as carbohydrates or proteins. By consuming more fat before their journey, it is readily available and is quickly transferred from the cells where it is stored into the blood stream for oxidation in muscle.

The light factor stimulates the pituitary gland found at the base of the brain. When the light penetrates the pituitary gland, it begins a series of hormonal triggers. The hormones secrete into the blood stream and begin a chain of activity to the ovaries, testes and other body organs. When this takes place, the urgency of migration is so intense that nothing can stop it.

Darwin quotes an example of an Audubon's goose that, when deprived of its pinion feathers, started the journey by walking on foot. He then goes on to describe the sufferings of a bird penned up at the time of migration, "which would flail its wings and bloody its breast against the bars of its cage." In *The Descent of Man,* Darwin notes that "in certain birds, the migratory impulse is stronger than the maternal. "A mother will abandon her fledglings in the nest rather than miss her appointment for the long journey south."

I read in *Escape* magazine that in some humans, a new gene has been located that is stronger and/or missing in others. When present, this triggers the need for adventure, exploration, and travel.

Bruce Chatwin in his book *Songlines* said, "What I learned there – together with what I now know about Songlines – seemed to confirm the conjecture I had toyed with for so long: that Natural Selection has designed us – from the structure of our brain-cells to the structure of our big toe – a career of seasonal journeys on foot through a blistering land of thorn-scrub or desert."

Man's movement can never compare to a bird's migration, but I know that I too have felt the restlessness and need to venture far away from home. And while the bird's migration is necessary and urgently connected to its survival, I must agree with a Moorish proverb. "He who does not travel does not know the value of man."

Fear, bigotry, and hate can only take place when a person stays in one place too long.

The Spark of Birding

America's fastest growing hobby has 65 to 76 million Americans hooked on birds.

For some, this may involve simply feeding the birds in their gardens, but for many, bird-watching is a sport, whether they're weekend bird watchers or hard-core birders who will drop everything – including the turkey on Thanksgiving Day – to chase a rare bird. There are also a growing number of inveterate birders whose insatiable appetites drive them to travel great distances to add numbers to their bird lists. Most fall somewhere in between.

What is the spark that starts the fire of passion for bird watching?

Some people will say it was seeing a particular bird for the first time. There is truth in that opening one's eyes and seeing a vivid living creature for the first time brings forth the wonder we felt as a child. For John Burroughs, it was a black-throated blue warbler that began his journey into nature. For Julian Huxley, it was a green woodpecker, and for radio broadcaster, John Kieran, it was an ordinary white-breasted nuthatch.

There is far more interest in birds in general than there ever was before the turn of the century. At that time, if a man was caught staring up into a tree at a bird, he must have been an embarrassed lad if not downright apologetic. Birds were to be shot – if not for the dinner table, to be stuffed and identified by the scientist seeking information, or to decorate a lady's hat.

Today so many people are lured outdoors if not by birds then by gardening. Outdoor sports such as hiking, biking, camping, and kayaking have launched a new need for more technical equipment and entrepreneurial endeavors.

As the world becomes more complicated, perhaps people need the simple comfort that mother earth unfolds. As children starve in some parts of the world and people continue to wage war because of racial and religious reasons, perhaps the insanity of it all causes us to yearn for the fundamentals, the earthly simple things – like a tiny bird.

Perhaps some would call it escapism. As Western humanity has built a gadget civilization in the search for convenience and comfort, we have also managed to insulate ourselves from nature. As Aldo Leopold referred to several political systems, including Communism, Capitalism, Socialism, and Fascism, they all ended up despising each other but their one creed was *salvation by machinery*. While we may enjoy the synthetic world we have created, we may detect that something is missing in this artificial world. Perhaps then, the pleasure of turning to nature can be understood.

As our forefathers pushed forward to build new frontiers, it is hard to imagine them taking time out to look at the loveliness of a sky filled with snow geese or listen to the eerie call of loons on a lonely lake at sunset. When survival was the issue, few had time to ponder or observe with wonder what they were busy assaulting. The hobby of bird watching had to wait for a time when life settled down to civilized intricacies.

It seems when life is more restrained, bird-watching takes flight.

Possibly, birding has become a way for civilized humans to pursue a primal need. *Homo Sapiens* are predators, and in the beginning, it was hunt or be hunted. Primitive man picked up the club to survive.

Though today we go to grocery stores to buy our meat, most of us never come in contact with our past predator selves. Maybe bird-watching takes us outside and allows us to hunt with binoculars instead of shooting a gun. The treasure becomes the bright feathered jewels we see through our binoculars and add to our lists.

Whatever it is that sparks the bird-watching passion, millions of people have discovered the need to connect with nature through birding.

And these same millions of people will be the first ones to make the commitment to save our planet.

Of Flight and Fantasy

One of North America's first environmentalists, Thoreau, once arrogantly said, "Since men could not fly, they could not contaminate the sky."

Fortunately, or unfortunately, depending on how you see it, the Wright Brothers proved him wrong. Humankind has not only contaminated this planet but has trashed the moon and airspace with discarded space remnants and satellites. We soon learned after we became airborne how to exterminate our enemies by dropping bombs.

The bird was probably the first animal we envied enough to try to imitate. Watching a bird take off from the ground so effortlessly and soar with ease in the sky must have awed early man. A bird ascending to the sky must have represented the ultimate freedom to his earthbound watchers.

Now we can fly faster, higher, and cover greater distances than our avian predecessors. A bird can only fly up to 175 to 200 miles an hour. And even though on a 1924 climbing expedition on Mt. Everest witnesses saw yellow-billed choughs flying as high as 27,000 feet, we have reached the stars in space.

However in comparing us to birds, we become laughable. Only a few birds such as the secretary bird and the California condor have difficulty getting off the ground, but then when they come down for landing they seldom have to be as careful as a plane does.

A Citabria (airobatic spelled backwards) can do loopy-loops and spins and whirl through the sky. But nothing can compare to a flycatcher that can leap to the sky from a perch, pick off an insect on the fly, and return effortlessly to his perch. Watch a swallow skim the glassy water of a still lake or turn directions in mid-air so fast that sometimes the eyes of the watcher loses the bird entirely.

But conquering the skies was not enough. We marveled as we watched hummingbirds hover over a flower, fly backwards and disappear from sight. Clumsy in comparison but functional, we earth bounders created the helicopter to hover in flight.

The Navy's famous Blue Angels fly tight formations, making maniac air maneuvers that excite and thrill the spectators. But nothing can compare with a Northern goshawk sailing through the forest trees at high speeds in chase of its hapless prey.

We watched ospreys dive perilously for fish, gulls fly by the wind and waves, and pelicans plunge headfirst and we created float planes to land and take off on water.

We watched and we dreamed that someday we too would fly. Out of the fantasy of flight, we took off and soared into the skies. But the poetic splendor of flight will always be when we stand earthbound and watch a bird in flight.

The Primitive Instinct of Hunting

Hunting is a primitive instinct, and without it, I doubt bird watching would even exist.

Shooting birds was pursued by biologists, artists, and scientists in the past. They did not have binoculars, and the only way to study in detail and paint a bird was to have the skin in hand. John James Audubon thought nothing of shooting birds and was a competitive shooter. I suppose that in the early nineteenth century, the sheer numbers of birds seemed inexhaustible.

When asked why I enjoy bird watching, I often reply that as a child, I liked collecting the colored glass I found on the beach. These precious pieces of glass became rubies, emeralds, and diamonds.

As an adult, I still enjoy the hunt, but treasures are now my jewels of the bird world. I "collect" them by adding their names to my bird list and nothing is killed.

Today, a hunting license is required to shoot birds, and there are restrictions as to what species a hunter can shoot. However, most people today in North America have a regard for the "reverence for life."

I remember as a child trailing after my father when he went out to hunt mourning doves. I hated the blast of gunfire and watching the bird fall from the sky. My father insisted we eat the tiny dove breasts that my mother hated to prepare. Eventually he gave up hunting completely as his respect for life grew. And my guess is he probably threw back most of the fish he caught.

Hunting with binoculars can be just as rewarding. It took me a long time to see a mountain quail, a flock of red crossbills, and a covey of chukar. When a rare bird has been found, the reporter trembles anxiously until someone with experience confirms the find.

Once the primitive instinct has been unleashed, a bird-watcher never views the world in quite the same way. Even if a birder takes out the trash, the eyes are watching and the ears are listening. A walk outdoors is never regarded as routine and becomes a moment of living in the present. A bird-watcher becomes one with his fellow friends, the deer, raccoons, squirrels and rabbits.

No one has to win at bird watching. The game is to watch and listen, wander and pause, sit and linger. A bird-watcher always enjoys never knowing what is around the next corner or what might be hidden in the branches of a tree. The illusion that something special or rare is lurking nearby is what drives the obsessive bird-watcher to the hunt and he or she will usually return with some trophy, even if it is a bird's feather or a pocket full of shells.

I am indifferent to the competition of bird watching. In the field, I will always defer to the more competitive and skilled birders. But birding has given me joyous moments and without the joy of the hunt, I would not have remembered seeing thousands of flamingos in Africa. I would not have seen the California condor soar across the sky at sunset, and I would not have seen thousands of scarlet ibis fly into roost at sunset in Trinidad.

My travels would not have taken me to Mai Po Swamp in Hong Kong, to the rain forests of Central America, or to the Atherton tablelands of Australia. The primitive instinct of hunting is now an endless joyous search.

The Graceful Art of Flying

Once mankind mastered the art of flying by applying the principal of thrust and lift, we built more powerful and faster flying machines – capable of moving faster than the speed of sound and journeying to the moon – faster and further than any bird on earth.

But our superior "flying machines" lack the grace and maneuverability of a fragile bird's wing. An airplane's wing is rigid, designed to conform only to high and low speeds – but a bird's flexible wing has the ability to fly fluidly, changing constantly and continuously.

Like its relatives the shearwaters and albatrosses, the northern fulmar is a powerful flyer with strong, stiff wings but lacks the smooth maneuverability of the gulls. Living at sea, the northern fulmar holds its wings rigid and soars like an airplane, alternating wing beats then gliding low over the waves.

The northern fulmar can fly like this because in contrast to the gull, its wings and body are narrow, its neck does not protrude, and its tail is short – all meaning less surface to catch the wind. Its wedge shape, broader in front, is due to the large pectoral muscles it needs for power flying.

Living on the ocean and far away from land, the fulmars, albatrosses and shearwaters must all be powerful flyers to survive.

Gulls, on the other hand, fly leisurely – and many times, I have watched them soaring high in the sky in circles without any apparent reason other than the sheer joy of flying.

When the wind picks up and blasts the coast, the gutsy gulls take off in the gale. California, western, and ring-bill gulls mix and match wits with each other, sweeping and swirling in a maze of confusion, speed – and near misses.

And as I stand watching them play tag with each other, I can't help remembering what Jonathan Livingston Seagull said, "That it is the right for a gull to fly, that freedom is the very nature of his being, that whatever stands against that freedom must be set aside, be it ritual or superstition or limitation in any form."

The Lure of the List

What is it that causes people to become obsessed with chasing birds? I have had many friends go bird watching with me and most of them never caught the bug, with the exception of our friend Ann, who now has more birds on her life list than my husband and I have.

One of the reasons I became interested in bird watching is I thought it was non-competitive. Having no interest in participating in most sports and certainly no interest in being a spectator, bird watching appealed to me. In sports, someone had to win and that meant someone had to lose, and in a perfect world no one should have to win at the pain of another person losing, or so I thought.

Seeking the pleasure of being outdoors by myself or with a group watching birds seemed civilized to me. No one had to lose.

At first, almost every bird I saw was new to me. I soon found myself putting a check mark in the bird book next to every bird I saw. Each outing was exciting because I invariably came home with something new. The lure of the list had me anticipating what new birds I would be able to check off on my next bird trip.

As it happens when birders persist long enough to see all the birds they can see, one day they will return home with no new life birds. Eventually, I began chasing rare sightings by listening to the hot line telephone recording. After a while, I began to travel to different areas in the United States to visit different habitats that attracted new birds, so I could check them off in my book.

I was still fascinated with the beauty and freedom of birds. I never tired of seeing some species over and over. For me, the game of bird watching is a treasure hunt, and these bright-feathered creatures were the jewels. The game was in the seeking.

I realized one day as I ticked another check mark in my book that I was keeping score in my game of bird watching. As in most sports, the scoring of the game is the exciting part to the players.

Horrors, did this mean I was competitive?

I rationalized that this certainly wasn't competitive since I was only keeping score with myself.

However, I was quite aware that some birders jostled for self-importance, self-esteem, and recognition from other birders in an extreme competition with each other.

Some wanted to have a higher count in North American birds than anyone else. The wealthier birders circled the globe in a manic search to add more species to their life lists. There were others who wanted to be the most knowledgeable in bird identification. Still others wanted to learn all the bird calls.

It seemed I had stepped into an arena of gladiators facing off. Bird watching did not seem so civilized to me after all.

In truth, the game of bird watching is an honor system. Some people prefer to find and see birds on their own. Others may hire a guide to take them to the birds. Some birders will check off a bird that is called out by an expert even though they never saw any detail other than just a bird flitting high in a tree or far out at sea. Since the player is the umpire, probably no sport has been abused more in the scoring of the game.

It wasn't until after I met my husband that I began to know my competitive side. I could go into a real funk if, at the end of a day, Dennis had seen a rare bird that I had missed seeing. The name of the game with a spouse is to stay even on a trip. Knowing how bad one would feel missing a bird the other one saw, we both worked hard at helping each other.

However, my most competitive moments are when I think about our friend, Ann, who 30 years ago went with us on a picnic and bird watching day. Since then, she has trudged through the rain forest of Ecuador, suffered the cold of Antarctica in search of penguins, and sailed the seas of Galapagos. Her world life list is a disgustingly couple of hundred birds over both of us.

And I never thought I was competitive.

About Yard Bird Lists

I was looking over our yard bird list this morning and found it to be quite impressive.

Of course, some might say we cheated when we moved half a block up the street and decided to continue the list we had started 30 years ago. To my husband and me, it was quite justifiable.

After all, it was still on the same street.

The yard bird list is defined by each birder who keeps one. Some of the more strict birders say that to count a bird on your yard bird list, the bird must actually be observed on the premises.

If we were to count just the birds seen on our property, our bird list would only be around 25 species. That means we couldn't have counted the golden eagle that flew over our house on September 20, 1981. We wouldn't have been able to count any of the hawks on our list, except the sharp-shinned hawk that has been hanging around lately, frightening all the small birds away from our bird feeders. Nor could we count the great blue heron, common merganser, double crested cormorant, belted kingfisher, or the swallows or swifts that we see fly overhead each spring and summer.

One of the more entertaining yard birds was observed one summer evening while we relaxed in our swing in the back yard. I looked up to see a huge bird land in the tree in front of our house. I ran for the binoculars. To our amusement and delight it turned out to be a wild turkey hen that stopped for a few minutes rest before taking flight again, and we added another new species to our yard list.

ABOUT YARD BIRD LISTS

The best yard birds, of course, are the rare birds that stop at the feeders for a short time. Dennis was able to count a white-throated sparrow on October 29, 1994. I was working at the taffy store when he called to report the bird to me.

Then there was the day, June 1, 1995, when I came down to eat lunch and saw a male rose-breasted grosbeak at the feeder. Dennis wasn't home, and when he returned and I told him what I had seen, he spent two hours staring out our kitchen window. The next day the bird reappeared – and I was back in my husband's good graces.

Of course, Dennis and I do sometimes disagree about the ground rules regarding what we can call a yard bird. One morning, we took a walk together and located a flock of red crossbills up on the ridge of the hill behind our house. We had a long discussion regarding the addition of this species to our yard list. Apparently, all my honest protestations went unheard, because red crossbills are definitely on our yard bird list.

Our adored and Northern California late bird leader Rich Stallcup once told my husband, "A yard bird is any bird that is seen while hanging with one arm holding onto the fence on the property."

With a total count of 73 species that I refuse to give up because of a move down the street, or my husband's over-exaggeration, maybe we should rename our yard bird list to our "street bird" list.

Awakening the Senses

My neighbor stopped by for a short visit and upon leaving she noticed a small bird at the bird feeder and asked, "What kind of bird is that?"

I looked at her in amazement and answered, "That's a chestnut-backed chickadee. You've never seen one?"

Shaking her head no, she said, "What a sweet little bird!"

I pointed to another tiny bird that flew in to grab a sunflower seed. "That's a pygmy nuthatch."

I would expect my friend, a non-birder, not to know a pygmy nuthatch, but I was astonished to find out that in her 25 years of living in Cazadero, she had never observed a chickadee. I'm sure I'm guilty of not seeing the world around me in other ways, such as watching a great athlete perform an amazing feat in football, but to have never seen a chickadee seemed to me like walking through life blind.

Theodore Roosevelt was known for not having great eyesight, being the only president who is wearing glasses on Mount Rushmore. But he had an uncanny ability to hear and identify birds by their individual calls.

Bird watching begins as a pleasure, but in reality becomes a skill about embracing all the senses collectively. Birding is as much about the ears and intellect as it is about the eyes. Through Roosevelt's failing eyesight, he had learned the art of listening to the individual songs of the birds.

Experienced birders know that to sight and identify all the different warblers during a spring migration demands a level of concentration that alters the entire act of seeing. And a little luck must be thrown in, too.

When you study the warblers, it's easy to conclude you know nothing at all about these birds, and you never will. But if you begin with a few of the easier ones in your locality and learn their distinctions, you will be less discouraged.

Bird watching requires seeing, but it also relies on vision.

My husband taught me how to identify birds by the giz – which is an abbreviation of the word *Gestalt*, a German word from Psychology that interprets patterns. To see the giz of a bird means to be able to identify the bird by flight, by color, and by shape.

By learning to identify the giz of a bird, birding connects us not only to a history of the natural order, but to our human history of experience.

Many people I know have walked through a forest and not seen a thing except perhaps a squirrel. And is it any wonder when their walk was filled with constant jabber.

On the other hand, a bird watcher will see the gray discreet dipper at the water's edge. He will see the jay examining a pinecone. For him, the hawks and eagles fly overhead and the song sparrow sings in the willows.

To take a walk in nature and notice nothing is to be deprived of pleasure. All natural history must be learned by second hand, or not at all. Becoming aware of the natural world is not unlike a meditation.

Whether it's finding a rare sighting, or completing a Christmas Bird Count with friends, or taking time to jot notes down in a notebook, bird watching is about seeking a connection. And if not a connection with ourselves, we seek to find ourselves in their behavior – whether a territorial dispute or a mating squabble.

But in the end, we find that birds are not us.

We have hunted birds, poisoned their environment, kept them caged, and tamed them – and we have even helped usher several species to extinction.

But in doing so, we have found that birds still elude us and continue to soar in our hearts, awakening all our senses.

"One man may take a walk and scarcely see a bird; another, with him, sees or hears, perhaps, five and twenty species." A.J.R. Roberts, *The Bird Book*, 1903.

Hollywood, Get it Right

The darkness blending with the stillness was unnerving.

I could smell the dampness in the air, and the coolness of the early morning embraced me, making me feel small and insignificant as I sat waiting in anticipation.

We were sitting in a rainforest just outside of Cairns, Australia and it was four in the morning. Why were we there? So we could hear what a rainforest in Australia sounded like when it awakened in the early morning hours.

The blackness began to fade into gray, displaying shadows taking form and shape as the early morning light began to steal its way into the dawning of a new day. At last I could see my husband near me.

Suddenly, the first call exploded with hysterical laughter rising with a staccato sound of *kook-kook-kook-ka-ka-ka,* causing my heart to pound in my ears almost as loud as the sound.

"What was that?" I whispered. Dennis gazed back at me in wonder. "It sounds like an old black and white Tarzan movie," I declared.

Our Australian birding friend grinned at me with a knowing look and said in his colorful accent, "That, my dear, is the call of the laughing kookaburra."

How did a laughing kookaburra from Australia end up here in a Tarzan movie, I wondered? Since I was a small girl, I always thought that call was a monkey in the deepest dark jungles of Africa.

For years I have been listening to my husband rave in outrage and protest when watching a movie on television. "Why do they do that? Here the movie is a setting in the mountains, and I'm hearing a meadowlark that lives in the grasslands singing in the background. Don't these guys who make movies know anything about the natural world?"

I must agree with him. It breaks the mood of the film to hear a bird or animal call that doesn't fit the setting.

Bird watchers are sensitive to the Hollywood's mistakes. For years, directors filled their movies with background sounds that didn't belong. I must give them credit though. The mistakes have been fewer in the recent past years.

Fewer, but still annoyingly present.

One evening, I was watching the movie *Waiting to Exhale.* There was a scene of a fake woodpecker making a wrong call that didn't belong in the desert. Was it necessary to show a nonexistent, animated woodpecker? Why not just leave it out?

In the movie *Just Cause,* with Sean Connery, there is a scene in a Florida swamp. In the background, tropical birdcalls from Central and South America fill the air. Any traveling birder would know immediately what a Florida swamp sounds like – and it isn't the same as a rainforest in Central or South America.

I remember renting an Australian flick and watching it all the way through even though it was a terrible movie. The reason I stuck with it was because it was set in an Australian rainforest, and I was enjoying the remarkably loud calls of the eastern whip birds.

The male's long drawn-out explosive whip crack is followed immediately with the female's answer. One will never forget this duet. This bad movie's only redeeming quality was that it was filled with accurate and exciting birdcalls.

Hollywood, take notice of the environment that surrounds you when making a movie. There are many bird watchers and wildlife naturalists that know when you have blown it. What works in a studio doesn't always work in a certain habitat.

Name Changes, Splits, and Lumps

Several years ago, my husband and I packed a picnic and headed for Pine Flat Road, Audubon Sanctuary, to celebrate our wedding anniversary. Our conversation quickly became argumentative when I spotted and called out, "Marsh hawk."

Dennis corrected me, "It's been called a northern harrier now, dear, for several years."

"I know," I replied, "but for me it will always be a marsh hawk."

Later during our picnic, I heard the distinct whistle of the western flycatcher, and called out, "Western flycatcher."

Dennis sweetly reminded me, "It's now called the Pacific slope flycatcher. They split the Western flycatcher into two species. Ours is the Pacific slope; the Sierras divide the territory for the other one, the Cordilleran flycatcher."

"That's right," I answered. "It's always nice to gain a species instead of having them take away a species from our lists. However, it will always be the western flycatcher for me."

Nibbling on a piece of chicken, Dennis pointed out a brown towhee and called out, "California towhee."

My feelings were beginning to feel as wrinkled as my brow when I replied, "It's still a brown towhee to me."

Dennis patiently explained. "The brown towhee has become separated."

"Separated from what?" I declared.

"It's now two species, the California towhee and the canyon towhee." Dennis continued to pontificate, "And that's not all. They have split

155

the rufous-sided towhee into two species, and the other one is now the spotted towhee."

"Oh, good grief! Who are these guys anyway and how do they get off making all these changes?" I demanded, clearly out of patience.

Dennis continued to explain that "they" were the American Ornithological Union, and they meet every few years to decide what birds needed name changes, lumps, or splits.

"Did you know that they have again split the northern Oriole into its constituent forms, including the black-backed oriole of central Mexico and the Bullock's oriole from the Baltimore oriole?" Dennis lectured.

I gave him a bored look and gazed up at the sky. Suddenly, I saw a white-tailed kite hovering. Perking up, I pointed and called out, "White-tailed kite."

Dennis, clearly trying to make me feel better, said, "You got that one right, Sweetie. They changed the name recently from the black-shouldered kite to the white-tailed kite."

"That's because I never changed the name in the first place," I squealed in exasperation. "Back some 20 years ago, it was called the white-tailed kite. And then your group of old fuddy-duddys changed the name to the black-shouldered kite. I never quit calling it the white-tailed kite and finally, they recognized their mistake of changing the name in the first place, and returned it to the original name," I announced triumphantly.

Dennis smiled and picked up his wine glass and toasted me. "To your stubborn disposition. I wouldn't have you any other way. Happy Anniversary, Baby."

Grinning sheepishly, I toasted him back, "Happy Anniversary."

Who Says Bird Watching Is Safe?

I stood gazing upwards with my binoculars to my eyes, so excited I could scarcely breathe. I was looking at my first pair of red-headed woodpeckers. The male had a snow white belly and blue-black back that gave contrast to its brilliant red head, throat, and neck – a smashing bird to see for sure.

Meanwhile, I kept backing up to relieve birders' neck – pain from looking upwards. Suddenly, I felt the ground give way, and I was falling down a hole like Alice in Wonderland. I landed at the bottom of a a five foot hole. My husband turned around to say something to me and was startled when he realized I wasn't there. "I'm down here," I said. "Help me up."

Then there was the time my husband ran off the road into the sand, and we had to be towed out because he was watching a bird and not the road. One time I had to run for my life while bird watching when a rogue wave hit the beach in Hawaii.

Even some of our leading and first ornithologists have had some harrowing experiences.

Ralph Hoffman, author of *Birds of the Pacific States,* lost his life on the California coast when he fell from a seabird cliff. In his mid-sixties, Herbert Brandt suffered a heart attack while scaling a wall in an Arizona canyon to investigate a flycatcher's nest.

Author of the famous *Life Histories,* Arthur Cleveland Bent, had trembling handwriting not because of his age but due to an accidental fall from a barred owl's nest. He luckily saved himself from the fall by lodging his arm in the crotch of the tree, but while hanging helpless, his fingers' nerves were permanently damaged.

Oology, the collecting of eggs, is a dead hobby now. But during its heyday, many collectors lost their lives while attempting to scale cliffs for eggs. And there is a recording of a group of falconers who peered over a ledge on the Hudson River and were shocked to see a dead body sprawled below. They later identified it to be one of their detested competitors.

Several other adventurous ornithologists, including the famous bird artist George Miksch Sutton, and Edward Howe Forbush, had close calls chasing birds.

But my favorite story about the dangers of bird watching is the story written by Eric Hosking, the first and foremost bird photographer, in his book *An Eye for a Bird, Autobiography of a Bird Photographer.* He climbed a tree to photograph a tawny owl on her nest. Suddenly, the owl became protective of the nest, and with lethal speed and deadly sharp talons, removed one of Hosking's eyes.

It must have been exciting to live in an era in which new species could be found nearly everywhere on our planet earth, or to be the first photographer to snap a particular bird, or to collect eggs for scientific study.

New species are still being discovered occasionally today, but the day of discovering vast numbers of species is over. But to the bird watcher, the adventure and discovery is at its highest in the beginning because everything he sees is new.

Birds have wings, and our hearts soar with passion as we discover them for the first time.

But we don't have wings, and it's wise to keep in mind the cautionary tales above – bird watching can be unsafe.

To Shed a Tear

*E*very time I hear the collision of a bird hitting our window, I shed a tear.

Holding a broken bird in the hand as it takes its last breath brings out compassion in anyone who loves wild creatures.

I once watched a female hummingbird invest days of energy to create a dainty woven nest and produce two tiny eggs the size of jelly beans. Each day I would get on the ladder and climb up to take a look. Finally one day, the eggs hatched, and two wet and blind baby birds, without feathers, sat with open mouths. The next day, to my anguish, the nest had been destroyed, and the chicks were gone. I discovered a rat the following night coming back to the scene of the crime.

We are all horrified to hear of tragedies involving the loss of thousands of birds.

In the book, *Birds of Minnesota* by Thomas S. Roberts, an unforgettable account is told. During a wet and heavy snowstorm in March, flocks of Lapland longspurs became confused, and many of them died by colliding with other birds and obstacles. An estimated 750,000 carcasses were found on just two snow-covered lakes. Roberts believed, the estimated millions of birds probably died in a 1500 square mile area. Evidently the birds showed no decrease in population, and were able to sustain the high loss. Maybe heavy losses of longspurs have occurred several times in the past.

High numbers in bird losses can generate astonishment and fear in us, but Nature seems to keep the balance in check. Dense population numbers of birds result in disease, fewer nesting sites, and more competition for food. In addition, birds fly into trees and mountains, as well as human-built towers and buildings. But in spite of heavy annual losses, almost all birds seem to produce an overage in their population every year.

However magnificent their survival powers are, birds still need a healthy habitat to survive – including suitable food, water, and nesting sites. But if their habitat is destroyed, the basis of the birds' existence has been annihilated and their populations threatened. When this happens, birds silently disappear, with no piles of carcasses to dramatically demonstrate the disaster.

Our herculean efforts to keep the California condor from extinction would not be necessary if the condor had not first lost habitat in its competition with ranchers and tract homes. The whooping crane would not be dependent on our attempts to bring back their numbers if we had not used their habitat to grow wheat. And passenger pigeons, the most abundant bird on earth, would not be extinct if man had not broken the successive nesting areas that were essential to its survival.

Still, tears will always well up in my eyes when I hold a delicate bird and watch it die in my hand. And I will always be horrified when I hear about an oil spill that has killed massive numbers of ocean birds and animal life. Only through our compassion and reverence for life may we be able to help them sustain unnecessary losses.

Sadly, our greed – and our need for more development – still exceeds our compassion for these beautiful creatures.

All or Nothing

I have a picture in my head that I have never seen, nor will I in my lifetime. That picture is now put down only in words for us to remember.

It is the spring migration of passenger pigeons moving north at winter's end.

Imagine millions of birds in both solidly massed and loosely flocked flights streaming northward. Some say the flight took as long as a day or longer before it was quiet again. Their massive concentration of numbers was several miles long, and the depth of their numbers cast a shadow on the ground. Domestic animals reacted to this sudden invasion from the heavens much as they do during the rumbles of earthquakes.

Durward L. Allen said, "The roar of the millions abraded the ear for hours; the air was filled with the sharp smell of them, and their dung spattered like hail on the leaves."

Native to North America, passenger pigeons were considered a nuisance, invasive mobsters, by many. Restless, rowdy, and noisy, the gregarious birds survived through the sheer weight of their numbers.

In winter in southeastern states, the pigeons would roost in high concentrations in forested areas. During the day, they flew together *en mass* to forests, where they took advantage of abundant acorns, chestnuts, and beechnuts. The forest floor was littered with guano after their departure. Their constant movements and flutter of wings must have been an awesome sight. During the evening, the long streams of birds would head to their roosting areas.

These birds took a toll on any territory they claimed as their own – and a forest or swamp showed the expense for many years. Birds piled on top of birds caused whole trees to lie flat on the ground. Most of the trees were fractured and dead. The ground underneath was buried in broken limbs and guano.

But like the caribou of the Arctic range, passenger pigeons knew when to move on, allowing the land to regenerate. If they had stayed as residents, they would have exhausted their food, polluted the environment, and probably have succumbed to disease.

John Burroughs said, "It was such a spectacle of bounty, of joyous, copious animal life, of fertility in the air and in the wilderness, as to make the heart glad. I have seen the fields and woods fairly inundated for a day or two with these fluttering, piping, blue-and-white hosts. The very air at times seemed suddenly to turn to pigeons."

Their nesting range extended from the Lake States to New England and north into Ontario, Canada. Like everything else they did, their nesting conformed to their need of numbers. Wherever there were mass amounts of food, nesting locations could be found.

Bela Hubbard, naturalist, geologist, author, and surveyor, describes, "A stretch of forest 16 miles long and 3 miles wide – 50 square miles with every suitable bough occupied by a dozen nests." The nesting area chosen would be occupied for approximately one month, and almost at the same time, the birds would depart leaving the forest alone for many years before being invaded again.

These huge concentrations of birds naturally attracted several predators, but their numbers were so huge the few taken were hardly noticed.

That is until the white man introduced the gun. Over the years of systematic slaughter, the gun's efficiency grew.

During the 1860s and '70s, the birds were murdered while roosting and in flight. The numbers taken increased every year. Their breeding cycle disturbed, the birds were reduced in number even faster. By the early 1900s, only a few stragglers were reported.

The last passenger pigeon faded from fact to fiction in 1914 when it died in a Cincinnati zoo.

Had the pigeons been able to exist in pairs, like the mourning doves, their species may have continued, but they could not. The passenger pigeons' need to live together in an extensive mob scene doomed the bird to extinction.

The birds could live only under the formula of all or nothing.

"We do not need this little bird as much as we need the qualities required to spare its life." Deirdre Platt, age 16.

The Arrogance of Humankind

The great naturalist of the nineteenth-century, John Burroughs, once said, "Indeed, what would be more interesting than the history of our birds for the last two or three centuries? There can be no doubt that the presence of man has exerted a very marked and friendly influence upon them, since they so multiply in his society. The birds of California, it is said, were mostly silent till after its settlement, and I doubt if the Indians heard the wood-thrush as we hear him. Where did the bobolink disport himself before there were meadows in the North and rice fields in the South? Was he the same blithe, merry-hearted being then as now? And the sparrow, the lark, and the goldfinch, birds that seem so indigenous to the open fields and so averse to the woods – we cannot conceive of the existence in a vast wilderness without man."

John Burroughs is best remembered as a prolific writer of essays about natural history, and for his love for birds. I was stunned when I came across this early writing. The arrogance of man a century ago, thinking the birds were there because of man, was outrageous to me. John Locke once said, "If a tree falls in the forest, and there's no one there to hear it fall, did the tree make a sound?"

The same logic of a tree falling and not making a sound could apply to Burroughs' statement that until man came to California, the birds didn't sing.

And then I found this quote in a collection of early bird writers. "Why have not these monsters of the sky been appropriated to the use of man? How comes it that he who has subdued the ocean and cultivated the earth; who has harnessed elephants, and even lions, to his chariot wheels, should never have availed himself of the wings of the eagle, the vulture, or the frigate pelican?" John Mason Good, *The Book of Nature*, 1839.

I suppose 173 years ago, the vastness of our natural resources seemed unending. The early settlers must have thought nothing had value unless it was put to use. How frustrating it must have been to look up at these flying creatures and not be able to harness their capability of flight. To them, the only useful birds were the ones they shot and ate.

Today, one bird in eight are threatened worldwide. The list of endangered species changes daily adding more species.

I'm sure Burroughs and his good friend John Muir could not have predicted that in one short century, the world would be facing the early stages of a human-caused biotic holocaust that could leave the planet impoverished for as long as five million years.

The Carolina parakeet, ivory-billed woodpecker, heath hen, passenger pigeon, Labrador duck, and the great auk have all ceased to exist.

And only man in his arrogance believes he can bring them back through genetics. In a century, a blink of a wink in time, man's conceit has been the broad historical force causing these extinctions.

Among them – logging, habitat loss, the millinery trade, unregulated hunting, and bird collecting by amateurs and professionals.

Scientists calculate our world has lost approximately 600,000 species out of a planetary total of 10 million since the beginning of the holocaust that began around the year 1950. Burroughs' belief that the birds sang only for humankind was innocent arrogance at its best.

If he and John Muir were alive today to witness the destruction of habitat, lack of salmon in the rivers, and the loss of bird species, their tears for what modern man has done would fill a sea of shame.

Our Sacred Land

*W*hile practicing my daily yoga, I always begin and end my exercise with a bow. Sometimes when I'm outside watching a sunset or the sunlight coming through the redwood trees, I will clasp my hands together and bow.

The reason? I want to capture the awareness of the moment. It's my acknowledgment of participation with the Universe, the recognition of a perfect moment in nature and my connection to it.

If the spiritual dimension is absent in a human being, it accords their actions to treat a place as an object. Separating worship from nature is impossible.

We have always searched the cosmos for answers. Native Americans have long held the land as sacred, along with all its beings, animate and inanimate. All religions have taught us to honor nature. In the Islamic religion, destruction of nature is a rejection of God and faith and with that simple consideration, failure to protect nature is not religious.

The essence of Jewish spirituality is to acknowledge the unity of beings and to honor that acknowledgement by looking at the world with wonder. It's the personal ambition of the weekly spiritual meditative practice called the Shabbat.

In the Christian religion, Jesus' disciples asked Him, "What is the greatest commandment?" And He answered, "You shall love the Lord your God . . . and the second is like it: Love your neighbor as yourself." All of creation and future generations deserve our efforts to heal this planet.

All the organized religions have taught us that it's our obligation to be good stewards of our planet. However, theocracy has been far too busy saving individual souls and not biology, thus ignoring the inner core and soul of the planet. Religion has silently stood by while the economy has assaulted and destroyed beauty, nature, and health.

Because we know what we are doing to the planet, the issue becomes a moral one, not just an environmental crisis. The more superficial we become in accepting yet another clear-cut development or drilling for oil in the Arctic, the more vulnerable the land is to exploit. Our yawns and sighs of indifference give positive energy to corporate America to continue to pillage and plunder our resources and ignore global warming. We need to register our outrage and indignation every time a criminal wrongdoing is done, not our boredom.

"I am just primitive enough to hope that somehow, somewhere, a cardinal may still be whistling on a green bush when the last man goes blind before his man-made sun. If it should turn out that we have mishandled our own lives as several civilizations before us have done, it seems a pity that we should involve the violet and the tree frog in our departure." Loren Eiseley, 1963

The Choice to Contribute

The dark mornings of winter always give me silence to reflect. I like to wake up early and start the ritual of day – making the coffee, turning up the heat, and mostly going outside into the cold darkness to retrieve the newspaper. Standing outside in my pajamas, I'm always struck with the beauty of where we live and give thanks. Whether it's the fog appearing at the top of the trees, or watching the streaming silhouettes of crows cawing as they rise to another morning, I feel an emotional response to the simple beauty of just being there.

Unfortunately, not everyone seems to feel this way.

Back in 2003, the Bush Administration's sweep of both the Senate and the Congress fortified them into making an even stronger commitment to attack the environment. What can one nature lover do in the wake of this giant assault?

If we wanted to save our treasures, we must take time to act.

I vowed to continue to write to our politicians, donate money, and speak up at county and city commission meetings in defense of a greener world. I vowed to inspire non-voters to go to the polls by showing them the beauty of a Townsend's warbler or a bird refuge at sunrise. Remembering that it was two million voices and signatures that saved the Arctic the first time around, I didn't feel so alone.

I attended a Public Hearing at the California Regional Water Quality Control Board, regarding the possible adoption of an Order waiving waste discharge requirements for timber harvesting activities. In a shaky voice and with shaky knees, I spoke to the board over a microphone in front of some 100 people. I'm a writer, not a speaker, and I vowed afterwards to become a better speaker because we all need to speak out.

There's a Universal Law that we get what we give. By choosing to pick up a can on the road rather than tossing one out the window, we have chosen to contribute. By choosing to write a letter against drilling or logging in National monuments, we have chosen to contribute. By voting instead of not voting, we have chosen to contribute.

By participating in the choice of contributing instead of just taking up space, the rewards can be huge. The astronomer Harlow Shapley once wrote, "To be a participant is in itself a glory."

Of course, taking time to contribute can not only drain the hours from a day but drain the soul. There will always be lost battles that cause anguish. There will be times we must look inwards and realize we fall short.

In a world of six billion human beings, facing the fact that half of nature's species could be gone in the next century, I can be glad that I didn't have a child.

I can't imagine having to face that child and tell her about the beauty of the chortles of a yellow-breasted chat that she will never hear.

I can't imagine showing her photos of the tall sequoia trees that stood in my lifetime and not in hers.

I can't imagine telling her what clean air was like while she wears a face mask.

I can't imagine not wanting to contribute to keep her planet beautiful.

"That sadness at loss is our best first response. It should not be our only response. We know the world gives us life, beauty, and solace. We would be ungrateful if we failed to give back." Christopher Cokinos, from *Hope is a Thing with Feathers*

Birds and Spirituality

The documentary movie, *Winged Migration*, begins with the following words appearing on the screen.

"For eighty million years, birds have ruled the skies, seas, and earth. Each Spring, they fly vast distances. Each Fall, they fly the same route back."

The movie shows the birds' odysseys as they journey through incredible dangers, both natural and man-made. Human beings are shown as both allies and enemies. As I watched the film, I felt as though I had become one with these extraordinary brave little beings as they confronted their own survival or mortality.

Throughout human history, birds have been a source of inspiration. They have a powerful place in our cultures, as symbols of freedom and wisdom and spirituality. Nature holds the answer to all of life's mysteries, and birds have always provided universal principals and spiritual guidance for all religions.

A certain calm is required to watch birds – a restless or agitated being warns the birds away. Patience and quiet is the first order in bird watching, and this state soon becomes meditative. A birder knows when he goes out to seek birds that he is in search of slowing down. Before the humbling experience of actually seeing the bird being pursued, the usual rhythm of walking becomes one of stalking.

Lama Surya Das, a leading spokesperson for the merging of American Buddhism and contemporary spirituality, says, "People tell me bird-watching is one of the best meditations; they get very still and quiet and wait for any movement; it's like watching the mind."

A Buddhist friend of mine once said that Buddhism and spiritual encounter can be a walk down a path bird watching.

Birds have always had a prominent place in symbology. The ancient Persians symbolized the human mind-soul as a bird they called Karshipta. The ancient Pantheons regarded birds as celestial messengers.

The fact that birds lay eggs – from which life emerges – brought forth the idea of the cosmic egg. In the Kalevala, the national saga of Finland, a bird lays six golden eggs and one iron egg – the iron egg becoming our earth. The cosmic egg is mentioned in Greek mythology and in Hindus tan.

All ancient religions refer to birds as sacred, for example, the phoenix, the Egyptian ibis, golden hawk, and the white swan of eternity.

The Bribri, an indigenous group residing near Puerto Viejo in Costa Rica, believe there is spiritual significance in the migration and view the birds as spiritual birds that traversed the world. Early in the mornings, the Bribri elders chant songs dedicated to the birds, asking them to deliver the seeds they need to grow crops for their families.

Among the Pueblo peoples, ceremonies have always been the center of their cultural lives. Birds are considered spiritual messengers, deeply integrated into their traditions. In their Native languages are more than 200 species of bird names. More than 100 birds are essential to the Pueblo culture. The migrations of birds marked the change of seasons.

In the Bible, Jesus pointed to birds and declared, "Behold the fowls of the air: for they sow not, neither do they reap, nor gather into barns; yet your heavenly Father feedeth them."

Birds, feathers, and wings are quoted and used as similes in the Bible over and over again and used to convey safety, spiritual love, and protection.

Poet Coleman Barks wrote, "Birds represent our longings for purity and freedom and they carry messages of ineffable joy." Perhaps, through our adoration of birds, we are communing with God, sensing His fellowship and enjoying His creation.

Following adoration comes stewardship for the planet, as I have never met a bird watcher who hasn't ultimately become a protector of our Earth.

"Spirituality is like a bird: If you hold it too closely, it chokes, and if you hold it too loosely, it escapes." Israel Santr Lipkin

Why We Need Nature More Than Ever

I came to live part-time at the Russian River 35 years ago.

The lush green of the emerald forest called to some place inside me I had rarely felt before. Each time I departed to go back to the city, I felt as though I were leaving an important part of myself. Twenty-four years ago, my husband and I moved here permanently, and I began to understand that feeling that kept me returning to the river.

It's called sacred land.

I have waded the Russian River's tributaries and watched steelhead fingerlings scuttle past my toes. I have watched blue dragonflies dance over the pure water of Austin Creek as I floated in the creek. I have watched a doe bring her wobbly-legged fawns to the creek for a drink. I have observed river otters pirouette in the river, and squirrels pursue each other in the tops of trees.

I have celebrated that inter-connectedness with these creatures and have touched the soul of my spirituality in the Universe that can only be called sacred.

One of Webster's Dictionary definitions of the word *sacred* is "a respect or reverence accorded holy things; venerated; hallowed." My own personal definition is – that which we can not do without.

After September 11th, 2001, churches, synagogues, and temples were filled with people seeking solace. But equally filled with people needing refuge were our state and national parks, wilderness areas, and city parks. The idea of finding holiness in a church exclusively is incompatible with finding holiness through nature. And separating worship from nature is impossible.

All life is nature, and the church first created sin when man went against nature.

After September 11th, we saw our humanity open up to one another in a way we never had. People gave from their hearts as well as through their checkbooks. For a short period, we were all connected as one. That journey made us return to who we are and what we believe.

Some of us needed to make the journey through nature so we could remember the things we hold closest to our hearts, what we cherish and love.

Our planet is becoming smaller every day. If we could remember the days following September 11th, when we saw our humanity and connectedness with each other, we would be wise to realize that we must begin to live within our means.

We consume twice as much oil as any other nation. And during the Bush years, we embarrassingly walked away from the table to limit our fossil fuel emissions through the Kyoto agreements. The Arctic National Wildlife Refuge was barely saved so we could drill everywhere else in Alaska.

The Pentagon is pushing to exempt itself from some of our nation's most important laws that protect the environment and imperiled species, including migrating birds, whales, dolphins, and polar bears.

Some of our leaders say it's our patriotic duty to mine gold with cyanide at the headwaters of the Blackfoot River. They say we must log America's few remaining old-growth forests and build more roads. They claim we need to explore for gas in the Rocky Mountains. They say we need to do this for jobs, for defense, and yet, no one ever mentions profit.

These exemptions are not necessary for national security.

Many of us might argue that it's our moral duty and more practical to protect our treasures on this planet. Thick forests insure the oxygen we breathe. The Antarctic holds expansive fresh drinking water, and our vanishing rain forests hold cures and answers in pharmaceuticals that we might need to survive in the future.

But the best reason to preserve our resources? We evolved from nature. And without it, we will perish. We need a buzzing natural world to stay healthy – both physically and mentally.

I remember standing on top of a Mayan pyramid and looking down at an ocean of jungle. Rising above that green sea of tangled plants and vines stood other mounds that once were giant pyramids in an ancient and sophisticated society.

That civilization disappeared hundreds of years ago.

What used to be fields of farmlands and cities with garishly-colored temples was now buried beneath the rain forest. And I remember thinking with great pleasure that nature would be there long after we are gone.

Nature doesn't need us to survive, but we need nature.

Author Bio

Pamela Conley is a writer and avid bird-watcher who formerly worked as a flight attendant for eighteen years and a weekly columnist for the *Bodega Bay Navigator* for twelve years, where she regularly wrote about bird and wildlife issues.

Author of *Vignettes of a Birder,* Conley has had her writing included in three anthology collections printed by Traveler's Tales Publications and has also been published in more than fifty magazines and online publications. Visit her at www.ChukarTales.com

www.ingramcontent.com/pod-product-compliance
Lightning Source LLC
Chambersburg PA
CBHW060301290526
45789CB00001B/371